EVERY WEEK MATTERS

Practical Strategies to Move Your Ministry Forward

Trevor Hamaker

DOWNLOAD YOUR BONUS MATERIAL

To say thank you for your purchase, I'd like to send you the FREE Bonus Material that goes along with this book. It includes dozens of templates and tools to help you create momentum, reach students, and grow faith in your ministry.

Download your FREE Bonus Material at:

www.betteryouthministry.com/everyweekmatters

Contents

INTRODUCTION

I didn't set out to become a youth pastor. The church had needs, and I was a willing volunteer. Sometimes they needed an extra helper for Vacation Bible School. Other times, they needed a substitute Sunday School teacher. I stepped in to serve in whichever roles were needed. My desire was to make a difference, and those opportunities gave me a way to do that.

During my junior year of college, while at home for winter break, my pastor suggested that I consider going to seminary. I liked the idea but wasn't entirely convinced I should do it. I hadn't been a Christian for very long, and my only experience was as a volunteer in various ministries. I liked church but had my doubts about working at one.

When I went back to school that spring, my friends were starting to apply for internships in their respective fields. It dawned on me that I should do the same. Even though I was pursuing a degree in Business Administration, I started looking for internships at churches.

You're Hired

I found a church in northern Virginia that was hiring an intern for the summer. It was a small church. They didn't have a youth pastor during the school year, but they hired someone every summer to keep their ten students occupied and out of trouble. That summer, they decided that person would be me. I still remember the phone call. The pastor told me, "We want to hire you to be our summer intern. Your budget is $250. See what you can do with that."

I made many missteps but learned a lot at that little church. Perhaps the most important lesson I learned was that what you say and what people hear you say can be very two different things. Let me explain.

One night, I was teaching the students about honoring their parents. When I finished, a girl named Stephanie was crying.

"What's wrong?" I asked.

Through her sobs, she explained, "When my mom left for work today, she told me not to watch more than two movies. She wanted me to go outside and do stuff. But I watched three movies today."

"Aww, that's alright," I reassured her. "Just tell your mom what happened. I'm sure she'll understand. There's no need to cry about it."

She said, "I think I'm going to hell."

"Why would you think that?" I asked.

Her reply? "Because that's what you said."

For the record, I never said anything remotely close to that. I never even mentioned hell. But somehow, that's what she heard in my message that night. Eventually, she settled down, and I was able to clarify what I wanted the students to hear. The lesson, however, was etched in my mind: There's a difference between what you say and what students hear you say.

RAISE YOUR EXPECTATIONS

The next summer I had another internship. This time, I worked at a much larger church in my hometown. At that time, they taught theologically-rich sermons, oversaw an amazing team of adult volunteers, and had over 400 students attending each week. Those three things are still true of that ministry today, by the way.

At that church, I had two jobs:

1. Plan and lead the middle school guys' Bible study on Tuesday mornings from 10:00-12:00.

2. All other duties assigned by the Youth Pastor.

It was a great learning experience to see how that church operated compared to the smaller church I had helped the previous summer. My key takeaway came when I asked the Youth Pastor what they were doing that made their ministry so successful. He said, "We have really high expectations of our students. We call them to do more and dream bigger than they ever thought they could. Their sports coaches do that. Why shouldn't their pastors?"

Having played baseball for my college team, I knew what he was talking about. None of my coaches were satisfied with half-hearted effort. They taught us how to do things the right way and expected them to be done that way. But I had never considered that approach in a church. Nevertheless, here it was, playing out right before my eyes.

Years later, I would read Alvin Reid say something similar. Reid is a professor of evangelism and student ministry at Southeastern Baptist Theological Seminary who said, "Young people are not children finishing childhood; they're young adults preparing for adulthood, and they will rise to the bar we set for them."[1]

It's the same point that the youth pastor made to me: raise your expectations.

MORE TO LEARN

I followed my first pastor's advice and enrolled in seminary after I graduated from college. The classes challenged me, and the experiences strengthened me. I made some great friends and even met my future wife while I was there.

One of those friends worked as a youth pastor at one of the local churches. I volunteered to help him by leading a group of high school guys. One day, my friend received a phone call from another church in the area: "Do you know any good youth pastor candidates? We have an open position."

He said yes and immediately called me to ask if I was interested. I didn't know much about the church in question, but I told him that I was willing to check it out. A few months later, I was introduced as that church's new youth pastor.

It was a good fit. That church had never had a youth pastor before, and I had never been a youth pastor before. We both had a lot to learn.

I remember showing up for work on my first Sunday after being hired. I was looking for the youth Sunday School room so I could join them. However, the Sunday School Director had other ideas. She intercepted me and redirected me to another class. I told her that I was the new youth pastor, so I belonged with the students. She insisted that I wasn't a student, so I belonged with the adults. That happened for two more weeks before I was finally able to convince the senior pastor to intervene.

But I had a lot to learn too. After spending the previous summer at the big suburban church with high expectations, I immediately tried to mimic their style and strategy in my new context: a small rural church with low expectations. It didn't work very well.

Fortunately, I was flexible enough to make adjustments. Two examples will show you what I mean. First, when I challenged students to read the Bible, I was shocked by the responses from several of them that they didn't know how to read. So I did something I never thought I would need to do: I recorded myself reading the Bible, put those recordings on compact discs, and gave them to those students.

Another thing I didn't foresee was the apathy of the parents. I was accustomed to suburbia, where parents were involved in everything. They shuttled their kids everywhere they thought would be good for them. That wasn't the case in this area. Many of my students' parents weren't particularly interested in church, but the students wanted to come. So, on Wednesday nights, I showed up early and drove the church van all over town to pick them up.

Honestly, I learned how to be a pastor at that church.

The stories and the lessons could go on for days. There was the time when a parent of a student threatened me and threw chairs at me. There was the time when a girl confided in me that she was cutting herself. There was the time when a fight broke out between two guys in a small group. There was the time I challenged the students to get involved and ended up having to sing in the choir to prove my point. There was the time when a pastor told me that leaving his church was a mistake because I wouldn't amount to anything apart from him.

The churches have changed, but the lessons are many. Through it all, two things stand out to me above the rest. First, every week matters. Second, there's always more to learn.

EMPTYING MY CUP

Like I said, I did not set out to become a youth pastor. After all, who would seek out a job where the most common question you're asked is, "When are you going to get a real job?" Of course, you and I both know better than that. Working in youth ministry *is* a real job. But the question still persists.

No, I didn't think that I would give the last 15 years of my life to this amazing, exhausting, exhilarating, frustrating, satisfying, transforming work that we call youth ministry. But I'm glad I did.

This book consists of practical strategies that I've learned along the way. I have been fortunate to work at three different churches. Under my leadership, each of those youth ministries tripled in attendance. That doesn't mean that I always knew what I was doing. There were several times when I didn't have the first idea about what to do. I still don't have everything figured out, but I do think that I've figured *some* things out. And I want to share those things with you.

My hope is that I can save you from making the same mistakes I've made. I also want to help you save time and make a bigger impact than I've made. It's like Andy

Stanley says, "If you are one step ahead of anyone, you have something to offer to someone who is one step behind you."[2]

Within the North Point organization, we call this emptying your cup. Here's what that means: I can't tell you everything you need to know. I can't *fill your* cup. But I can tell you everything I know. I can *empty my* cup. When that happens, you will have the advantage of knowing what I've learned along the way in addition to what you've already learned. That combination will dramatically increase your opportunities for impact in the future.

That's why I wrote this book. And, if you think about it, that's what we're doing in youth ministry. We're ahead of our students in years, experience, and spiritual maturity. Because of that, we're able to point out the potholes and landmines that will prohibit them from reaching their destination. We're also able to point them toward the greener pastures and abundant life that they desire and Jesus offers.

Your students are better at life because you empty your cup every week. My hope is that you will be better at ministry because I'm emptying mine in this book.

READY TO GET STARTED?

If you're ready to move your ministry forward, it's time to get to work...

CHAPTER 1
WHAT'S THE MOST IMPORTANT THING A YOUTH PASTOR CAN DO?

The interview was wrapping up. As far as I could tell, I'd handled all of the search committee's questions with style and skill.

They were tasked with finding a new youth pastor for the church, and I felt like they had asked every question imaginable:

- How would you recruit new volunteers?
- Would you take students on an international mission trip?
- Should we split our middle school and high school students?
- Do you feel comfortable preaching in the adult service?
- How important is it to partner with parents?
- What do you believe about predestination?
- Why are you the best candidate for this job?

I felt good about my answers so far.

The next question was also the last question of the interview:

"What do you think is the most important thing a youth pastor can do?"

I don't know what they wanted to hear, but my answer seemed to surprise them. It might surprise you too.

KEYSTONE HABITS

I noticed something interesting about myself recently. When I work out and exercise, I avoid junk food. When I don't work out and exercise, I don't avoid junk food. Not only that, but I've noticed that when I stay active, I'm in a better mood, get to sleep more easily, and have more energy. That makes working out, exercising, and staying active a keystone habit for me.

The idea of keystone habits was made popular in Charles Duhigg's book, *The Power of Habit*. What is a keystone habit? According to Duhigg, keystone habits "are the ones, that, when they start to shift, dislodge and remake other patterns."[3]

When I'm active, that activity shifts my eating patterns. That's why it's a keystone habit.

In ministry, your relationship with God is a keystone habit.

TENDING TO THE STREAM

John Ortberg tells a tale about an old man who lived in the mountains and served as the Keeper of the Stream. Mostly unseen, he would travel from one spring to the next, removing debris from the water as he went.

One year, the town council decided to spend their money

elsewhere. Other things were seen as more important than taking care of streams that no one would see. Roads needed to be repaired, and buildings needed to be built. So the old man was relieved of his duties.

But, high up in the mountain tops, debris started to fill the springs. Trees fell and branches broke off into the water. Mud and silt accumulated. Further down the mountain, other waste contaminated the flow of fresh water.

For a while, no one seemed to notice. Life went on as usual. But after a while, the water wasn't the same. The clean water, with its refreshing sparkle, had gone away. In its place was water of a brackish kind that no one could enjoy.

The townspeople realized what they hadn't realized before: their lives were dependent on the stream, and the quality of the stream depended on the important work of the Keeper of the Stream. The city council reconvened, and rehired the old man. It wasn't long before the water was pure again.

Ortberg concludes the story by saying, "The stream is your soul. And you are the keeper."[4]

THE MOST IMPORTANT THING

The search committee had asked me a question that I hadn't expected: What do you think is the most important thing a youth pastor can do?

I answered, "The most important thing a youth pastor can do is stay close to God."

I wasn't trying to be spiritual; I was being serious.

They looked surprised, so I elaborated:

If I don't stay close to God, then this is all for nothing.

If I don't stay close to God, then my family won't respect me.

If I don't stay close to God, then the students will see through me.

My whole ministry depends on me staying close to God.

With that, the interview concluded. I received a call on the way home from the head of the search committee. He told that they loved my last answer and wanted to hire me to be their new youth pastor.

It's important for you to understand that your ministry is the overflow of your relationship with God. If you aren't filled with the truth of God and passionate about the love of God, then don't be surprised if your students aren't either. Your leadership in this area will set the tone for your ministry; students will follow your lead.

Your Move

In ministry, your relationship with God is a keystone habit. Don't allow it to take a backseat to programming and planning. As important as those things are, it's more important for you to stay close to God.

Block out at least an hour each week to read the Bible. Spend some time in prayer. Sing two of your favorite worship songs. Do whatever you need to do to encounter God in a personal way.

That time isn't wasted. You're investing in your own relationship with God because that's the most important thing you can do for yourself, your family, your students, and your church.

STRATEGY #1:

Stay close to God.

CHAPTER 2

THE TICKING TIME BOMB THAT WILL BLOW UP YOUR MINISTRY

When my kids are out of school for the summer, we like to take walks around our neighborhood after dinner. Well, I should clarify: my wife and I walk. My kids ride their bikes.

But one night, something crazy happened. My son was riding his bike down the road, and one of his pedals fell off! You can't ride a bike without pedals, so I tried to screw the pedal back on with my hand. No luck. Ist didn't work. I really needed a wrench to get it back on.

So, he had to walk and push his bike all the way back to our house. That was definitely not fun for him.

The whole episode got me thinking: A pastor without character is like a bike without pedals.

It just doesn't work. And yet, concern for character seems to get lost in the weekly rush of planning and preparing for the programs that keep our ministries going.

That's why a lack of character is the ticking time bomb

that will blow up your ministry. Your character is too important to leave to chance.

What Is Character?

We get our word "character" from the Greek word *kharakter*, which meant, "engraved mark" or "imprint."

But character is a slippery word to define. Before he offers his own definition of character, Andy Stanley observes, "In your pursuit of character, you will find many obstacles along the way. Defining it is the first one."[5]

What is the definition that he settles on? He says, "Character is the will to do what is right as defined by God, regardless of the personal cost."[6]

Or, how about this definition from Dallas Willard: "Character refers to the settled dispositions to act in certain ways, given the relevant circumstances."[7]

I've also heard it said that "Character is who you are when no one is watching,"

The theme in these definitions is that character has to do with your inner world: thoughts, convictions, will, intentions, attitudes, beliefs, and desires. Your character is the core of who you are.

How Is Character Formed?

Because character is so important, it's important to understand the ways that character is formed.

The way I see it, character is formed in three ways:

1. Head
2. Heart

3. Hands

With the head, we think. We direct our attention. And you know that when you give something your attention, you move in that direction. That's why it's so important to monitor your thoughts: "Fix your thoughts on what is true, and honorable, and right, and pure, and lovely, and admirable. Think about things that are excellent and worthy of praise" (Philippians 4:8 NLT).

With the heart, we feel. We experience emotion. But emotions can get you turned upside down and backward. That's why Andy Stanley counsels, "To become a leader worth following, you must give time and attention to the inner man. To leave a legacy that goes beyond accomplishment alone, a leader must devote himself to matters of the heart."[8]

With the hands, we act. We do things. We act on the hundreds of small choices that we make every single day. According to C. S. Lewis, "Every time you make a choice you are turning the central part of you that chooses, into something a little different from what it was before."[9]

Your character is always under construction. Your head, heart, and hands are the raw materials that are being used to build it.

How Pastors Blow It

A youth pastor confided in me recently that he hasn't *really* prayed in almost seven months. Sure, he's stood up on Wednesday nights and opened up the program with a prayer. He's ended the time with a prayer. But prayer hasn't mattered to him personally.

How does that happen?

He simply got caught up in the rush of ministry. He cared more about planning events than praying for students. He started to rely on his own gifts instead of God's grace. That's a formula for failure in youth ministry. It's a formula for failure for any pastor.

But we see it happen all the time, don't we?

I remember when I first heard about the Ted Haggard scandal. It caught me off guard. Haggard was a major leader in the Evangelical church at the time.

Not long ago, I came across a news story about two pastors in Tennessee who were arrested for soliciting sex with underage girls. One of them was a children's ministry director.

I've worked at a church where the senior pastor had a moral failure. I can tell you that it's not pretty.

Again, *how does that happen?*

I think pastors blow it for three reasons:

1. They stop listening to their own sermons.

2. They have limited (or no) accountability.

3. They are leading on empty.

First, they stop listening to their own sermons. They stop preaching to themselves. They are more concerned with delivering a sermon to others than applying it in their own lives. That's why they're able to say all the right things even when they're living in all the wrong ways.

Writing sermons is a skill, and they know how to do it well. The problem is that they are no longer practicing what they preach because they're no longer listening to what they say.

The second reason pastors blow it is that they have limited (or no) accountability. Being a pastor is very different from having a regular, 9-to-5 job. Trust me; I've done both.

In a regular job, you have a place where you're expected to be all day. There are tight controls on spending and expenses. But most church jobs aren't like that. There is tremendous freedom. You can come in late and leave early if you want. You can get reimbursed for expenses even if you forget to turn in your receipt.

Not only that but the higher up you go in a church, the less accountability there seems to be (at least that's how it seems to be in most of the churches I've been around). Excessive freedom and available funds create a strong temptation for a pastor without accountability.

The third reason pastors blow it is that they are leading on empty. In their book, *Pastors at Greater Risk*, H. B. London, Jr. and Neil Wiseman give these staggering statistics:

- 90% of pastors feel like they're not adequately trained to deal with the demands of ministry.
- 80% of pastors believe that ministry has a negative effect on their families.
- 80% of pastors say they have insufficient time with their spouse.
- 70% of pastors do not have someone they consider a close friend.[10]

Just let those statistics sink in for a minute.

It's no wonder that Wayne Cordeiro writes, "Most of the people in our churches have no idea how demanding ministry can be or even how demanding *they* can be."[11]

Pastors are burned out. They're leading on empty. And

that makes them susceptible to a great fall. That's a major reason why they blow it.

Ultimately, pastors who blow it forget what's at stake with every choice they make. Don't make that mistake. Your future – both personally and professionally – is on the line. Your legacy – how you'll be remembered and talked about – is up for grabs.

YOUR MOVE

Your character holds your ministry together. Without it, your ministry will be as good as a bike without pedals. So, your action step is to take an inventory of your head, heart, and hands:

How are your thoughts?

How are your emotions?

How are your actions?

What kind of person are you becoming?

Is there anything that gives you a reason to doubt your character today?

If you aren't listening to your own sermons, start. You need to do what you're telling everyone else to do.

If you don't have any accountability, you need to get some. A friend of mine calls this his "Blackmail Relationship." By that, he means that his accountability partner knows so much about him that he could blackmail him if he ever wanted to. Find someone (even if it's a professional counselor) and get real with them.

If you're drifting toward burnout, take a vacation. Find a hobby. Step away and do what you need to do to recapture your passion. Your family, students, and church need you to be burning bright with faith and passion, not burning out.

Perhaps the best thing any of us can do is pray the words that King David prayed: "Create in me a clean heart, O God. Renew a loyal spirit within me. Do not banish me from your presence, and don't take your Holy Spirit from me. Restore to me the joy of your salvation, and make me willing to obey you" (Psalm 51:10-12 NLT).

STRATEGY #2:

Keep watch over your head, heart, and hands.

CHAPTER 3
HOW TO BECOME A LEADER PEOPLE WANT TO FOLLOW

Tony Morgan says, "I think the true test of leadership is leading volunteers."[12] I think he's right.

One of the reasons why leading volunteers can be so difficult is that you aren't paying them. When you trade pay for performance, you have leverage in the relationship. If the person doesn't show up prepared or simply doesn't show up at all, you can fire that person and find their replacement fairly quickly.

It's hard to do that with volunteers.

When they email you at the last minute to let you know they won't be there, most of us just reply with a simple, "That's okay. See you next week."

When you see your volunteers looking over their lesson plans for the first time with only five minutes before the program starts, most of us just make light of it, and they offer a quick excuse.

We've all been there. And what option do we have to do it differently?

If you're at a larger church with a deep base of potential volunteers, I guess you could fire them (though you probably wouldn't call it that) and find a replacement. But most of the youth pastors that I talk with aren't in that situation. They're working with the small pool of people who have made themselves available.

Either way, whether you're at a large church or a small church, who among us hasn't wanted to let a volunteer go, only to realize that there isn't anyone else who is ready or willing to take that role right now? It happens to all of us from time to time.

So, What Do We Do?

We either let it go without a word, or we have yet another conversation with the same person about our expectations and their less-than-stellar performance.

There has to be a better way forward than that. One way forward is to become a better leader. You have to become the kind of leader that your volunteers want to follow.

Is that possible?

I believe it is.

What Do People Want in a Leader?

James Kouzes and Barry Posner have researched and taught leadership for over 30 years. They began their research by studying what people expect of their leaders. They started with an open-ended question: "What values, personal traits, or characteristics do you look for and admire in a leader?"

When all of the results were in, the list of several hundred different responses was distilled into a list of 20 characteristics. That shortened list then formed the basis for their updated survey aimed at identifying the exact traits most people admire in leaders.

Here's what's interesting:

For 25 years, they've given this same survey to over 75,000 people around the world. Over time, they discovered that only four of the characteristics have received over 60% of the votes across different countries, cultures, organizations, genders, educational levels, and age groups.

While every one of the characteristics received *some* votes, only four stood out from the rest. That means that what *most* people look for in a leader – a person they would be willing to follow – has remained constant over time.

What are those four characteristics?

Before I tell you, I want you to know that I have included Kouzes and Posner's survey in the Bonus Material for this book. I would encourage you to print it out and give it to your volunteers at your next meeting. Have them fill it out and talk about their responses together. I think it could spark some good conversations among your group.

Ok, now for the answer to your question…

4 CHARACTERISTICS OF LEADERS PEOPLE WANT TO FOLLOW

1. HONEST

Kouzes and Posner report, "In almost every survey we've conducted, honesty has been selected more often than any other leadership characteristic…Since the first time we conducted our studies, honesty has been at the top of the list."[13]

2. Forward-Looking

According to their research, Kouzes and Posner also found that "People expect leaders to have a sense of direction and a concern for the future of the organization…Whether we call that ability vision, a dream, a calling, a goal, or a personal agenda, the message is clear: leaders must know where they're going if they expect others to willingly join them on the journey."[14]

3. Inspiring

Kouzes and Posner observed that "People expect their leaders to be enthusiastic, energetic, and positive about the future…A leader must be able to communicate the vision in ways that encourage people to sign on for the duration and excite them about the cause."[15]

4. Competent

If you want people to follow you, they have to believe you know what you're doing. In Kouzes and Posner's words: "To enlist in a common cause, people must believe that the leader is competent to guide them where they're headed. They must see the leader as having relevant experience and sound judgment. If they doubt the person's abilities, they're unlikely to join the crusade."[16]

When these four characteristics are taken together, what emerges is a true foundation for your leadership: credibility.

Kouzes and Posner summarize their research by

concluding, "If you don't believe in the messenger, you won't believe the message."[17]

Without credibility, you won't be taken seriously as a leader.

YOUR MOVE

I want you to evaluate yourself as a leader. In fact, it would be a good idea to ask a few other people to evaluate you. Ask your coworkers, your volunteers, a few parents, and maybe even a few of your students to help you.

Do they see you as honest?

Do they see think you're forward-looking?

Do they believe you're inspiring?

Do they see you as competent?

If you want to become a leader that people want to follow, the results are in. These are the traits that people – including your volunteers – are looking for in a leader.

STRATEGY #3:

Invite others to evaluate your leadership abilities.

CHAPTER 4
HOW TO GROW AS A LEADER

For a long time, youth ministry was seen as a stepping stone. I don't know of any youth pastor that hasn't been asked by a well-meaning church member, "So, how long until you start working with adults?" Or, they'll ask, "How long until you become a *real* pastor?" That one really hurts!

Fortunately – thanks in large part to guys like Duffy Robbins, Doug Fields, and Reggie Joiner, along with ladies like Kara Powell and Kenda Creasy Dean – youth ministry is being taken more seriously today, and youth pastors are seeing their role as more significant than just a stepping stone toward becoming a *real* pastor one day.

There's No Place for Complacency

That doesn't mean youth pastors should become complacent. Just because you don't plan on becoming a lead pastor or a senior pastor one day doesn't mean you should rely on the talents and skills that brought you this far.

I wish this went without saying, but it doesn't. I know youth pastors who haven't read a book in over ten years. They're content where they are; they don't plan on going anywhere, so they don't see any point in developing their leadership skills or working on their ministry programs. They just keep doing the same things year after year.

Instead of taking the complacent approach, you have to take every opportunity you can to grow as a leader. That's true whether you plan to stay in your current church in your current role or move on at some point in the future.

In their book, *Great Leaders Grow*, Ken Blanchard and Mark Miller explain, "Growth brings energy, vitality, life, and challenge. The people I meet who aren't growing are also the ones who find life and their jobs boring. Without growth, we're just going through the motions."[18]

The contrast is stark:

If you make an effort to grow as a leader, you will be rewarded with positive results. If you don't grow as a leader, you will stumble along, complaining about all the things you can't change, until your influence eventually evaporates.

I think you would agree with that. After all, you're reading this. You want to learn. You want to grow. You want positive results.

But, how do you know what will actually help you grow and what is just a waste of time?

This list should help.

4 WAYS YOU CAN GROW AS A LEADER

1. GAIN KNOWLEDGE

Every leader might not be a reader, but every leader must be a learner. In particular, there are three areas in which you must gain knowledge:

a. Yourself. One of the best ways to learn about yourself is to take assessments. For instance, the StrengthsFinder Assessment is based on the work of Donald Clifton, Marcus Buckingham, and Tom Rath. It identifies the areas where you have a natural aptitude and will likely make your greatest contributions.

When I learned that my top 5 strengths are Input, Learner, Achiever, Belief, and Individualization, it brought clarity to why I approach people and tasks the way I do. I've been able to operate in my sweet spot more consistently because of what I've learned about myself.

b. Others. To be a leader, you must continually learn about the people you work with, as well as the people you're trying to reach. You can do this with a simple combination of personal conversations and observation. When you drive around your town, notice what's going on. When you interact with students, pay attention to what they say. When you talk with volunteers, listen for what's going on beneath the surface.

This is especially important when it comes to making people feel appreciated. For some, a gift card will do. For others, a handwritten thank you note means much more than a $25 gift card. It's important for you to learn who appreciates what.

c. Youth Ministry. You need to pay attention to trends that are happening in youth ministry. You don't want to invest money in projectors and screens when widescreen TVs will give you higher picture quality for a fraction of the price. That's a shift that has happened in the last few years. Many people who aren't paying attention are paying thousands of dollars every year to keep the old way going.

Invest in good resources, buy books, go to conferences, and work on your skills. You don't just want to be a good youth pastor. You want to be the best youth pastor in your town. The only way to do that is keep learning and gaining knowledge about the best practices in youth ministry.

2. REACH OUT TO OTHERS

As I share in *Your First 90 Days in a New Youth Ministry*, one of the best things you can do to grow as a leader is to visit other churches in your area. This accomplishes two things: you get to see what other people are doing, and you make some friends who are also in ministry.

Don't just show up announced, however. Send an email to the youth pastor a few days before you plan to show up. They'll appreciate the heads-up. When you visit another church, be sure to take notes on what they do well and what they do poorly. You're not in competition with those churches, but you can learn from what they're doing and how they're doing it.

If your schedule doesn't allow you to get to other churches because your ministry meets at the same times as theirs, that's okay. Give the other youth pastor a call and ask them to meet you for breakfast or coffee. Better yet, ask them if you can stop by their church and check out their student area. While you're there, talk to them about what's working and not working for them. The insights I've gained from those kinds of meetings are worth more than a ticket to a 3-day youth ministry conference.

Be sure to send a follow-up email thanking the person for meeting with you.

Also, don't forget about social media. You can follow other ministers and ministries to keep an eye on what's happening in your community and around the country.

3. OPEN YOUR WORLD

Blanchard and Miller suggest, "Be on the lookout for experiences inside and outside of work that will make you a better leader over time."[19]

Inside of work, you can open your world by:
- Having lunch with a coworker.
- Helping another ministry leader.
- Shadowing another pastor for a wedding, funeral, or hospital visit.

Outside of work, you can open your world by:
- Finding hobbies.
- Developing friendships.
- Saying yes to random opportunities.

I especially want to encourage you to say yes to random opportunities. So many times our default stance is to fall back into our regular routines. We say no to the things that could really open up our world. Say yes instead.

4. WALK TOWARD WISDOM

Proverbs 4:7 says, "Getting wisdom is the wisest thing you can do!" (NLT). But wisdom doesn't come overnight. It's a process, so be patient. Even so, there are two things you can do right away:

a. Get honest feedback. Ask the people who work with you to give you honest feedback to three questions:

- What should you start doing?
- What should you keep doing?
- What should you stop doing?

b. Seek wise counsel. Blanchard and Miller say, "Counsel is often derived from the experience of the person you're talking with. You get to benefit from their experiences."[20] Two key questions you can ask are:

- What do you know now that you wish you had known 10 (or 20) years ago?
- If you were me, what would you do?

Your Move

If you're serious about being a leader in youth ministry, you have to grow. Specifically, you have to:

- Gain knowledge.
- Reach out to others.
- Open your world.
- Walk toward wisdom.

In the words of Blanchard and Miller, "Your capacity to grow determines your capacity to lead."[21]

STRATEGY #4:

Get serious about personal growth.

CHAPTER 5

HOW TO INCREASE YOUR LIKEABILITY FACTOR

You want to be liked. I know you do. I know you do because I want to be liked too. We all do. It falls somewhere between levels three and four on Maslow's Hierarchy of Needs.

Sure, you don't have to be liked to be successful in youth ministry. But it's a lot more satisfying if you are.

What is likeability?

In its simplest form, likeability is the ability to create positive feelings in other people. In his book, *The Likeability Factor*, Tim Sanders offers a more sophisticated definition. He says, "Likeability is an ability to create positive emotions in other people through the delivery of emotional and physical benefits."[22]

WHY DIDN'T WE LEARN ABOUT THIS IN SCHOOL?

Unfortunately, likeability isn't something I learned about in school. Did you? I guess my teachers thought that left-brained "hard skills" would take me farther in life than right-brained "soft skills" would.

If only they'd seen the Columbia University study by Melina Tamkins. She discovered that people who were popular with their coworkers were seen as trustworthy, motivated, serious, decisive, and hardworking. On average, they received more pay increases and greater recognition for their efforts. Meanwhile, their colleagues who possessed a lower likeability score were perceived as arrogant, conniving, and manipulative. They had a hard time getting ahead no matter how hard they tried.[23]

It turns out, your success might actually be determined in large measure by how likeable you are. It's best to have both competence and likeability, but if you can only have one, it's better to be likeable.

I worked at a church where the previous youth pastor was asked to leave because he wasn't liked. He had a history of making humiliating comments to students. He thought he was being funny and provocative, but everyone thought he was just being rude and mean. He actually had good skills as a youth pastor, but people didn't like him, so he had to go.

Likeability is an important factor in your success in youth ministry. So, how can you increase your likeability factor?

7 WAYS TO BE MORE LIKEABLE

1. BE REAL

Communication coach Karen Friedman says, "If you want to be a likeable leader, start with being human."[24] People like people who are honest, authentic, and sincere. Lying, hypocrisy, and insincerity will ruin your relationships and your likeability.

2. RESPECT PEOPLE WHO AREN'T AROUND

Psychologists have discovered an interesting phenomenon called _Spontaneous Trait Transference._ Basically, when you're describing the person you previously worked for, or the attitude of the person who took your order at lunch, the people you're talking to project those same traits on to you.

In effect, what you say about other people is perceived as being true of you too. Therefore, you must be careful what you say about other people, especially when they aren't around to defend themselves.

3. BE GENEROUS WITH COMPLIMENTS

Leadership expert John Maxwell says, "The most fundamental and straightforward way of winning with people is to give them a compliment – a sincere and meaningful word of affirmation."[25]

We all have a hunger for attention, affirmation, and appreciation. Look for ways to encourage people with a compliment, and your likeability factor will be on the rise.

4. PAY ATTENTION WHEN PEOPLE ARE TALKING

I find myself in a lot of conversations with people who are distracted by other things. Sometimes it's their cell phone; other times it's a television in the restaurant. Either way, it's clear that they aren't interested in me and what I'm saying.

Don't be a distracted listener. Don't be an interrupter

either. Instead, follow the advice of David Schwartz: "Practice conversational generosity...Let the other person talk to you about *his* views, *his* opinions, and *his* accomplishments."[26]

5. Follow Up

Sometimes people share things with you that they're excited or worried about. If it's a student, maybe she's nervous about a big math test coming up next week. It could be a college acceptance letter that hasn't arrived yet. Maybe a grandparent is having health issues.

Whatever the case, when someone shares something that's on their mind, be sure to follow up with them after a few days. Doing so will communicate that you were really listening and that you really care.

6. Add Value

When you're really listening and paying attention to what someone is saying, you'll pick up on their wants and needs. Maybe a students' parents are going through a divorce. Who can you connect them with who has already walked that road?

Maybe you have students who have leadership potential. What are some resources or experiences you can give them to help them take the next step? If you help people get where they want to go, they can't help but like you.

7. Share a Meal

Whether it's Chick-fil-A, Outback Steakhouse, or your own house, something special happens when you share a meal with someone. Food can tear down walls of hostility among enemies and strengthen bonds of unity among friends.

In our hyper-connected culture, what's in short supply is human attention. Many people are starved for attention. Email is the dominant mode of communication because it's expedient, but it's also cold and dry. The phone is a little warmer because you can hear voice inflection and tone. The most effective mode of communication by far is face-to-face. Everyone has to eat, so why not share a meal with someone and get to know them better?

YOUR MOVE

Like I said earlier, your success is determined in large measure by your likeability. One of the best things you can do for your current and future students is work on becoming more likeable today.

I have included a Likeability Assessment for you in the Bonus Material. All you have to do is answer the questions, calculate your score, and start improving.

STRATEGY #5:

Increase your likeability factor.

CHAPTER 6

SMALL CHOICES THAT HOLD YOUR MINISTRY BACK IN BIG WAYS

We're all familiar with small choices that have big consequences after some time has passed. For example, eating fast food will hurt your health. Not immediately, but eventually.

I still remember the first time I saw *Super Size Me*, the documentary in which a guy only ate McDonald's food for thirty days. I was shocked by what I saw. If you've seen it, you know what I'm talking about. The man gained twenty-four pounds and had terrible mood swings throughout the entire month.

That's a small choice with negative consequences.

On the other hand, there are also small choices with positive long-term consequences. Changing the oil in your car is an example. You could keep driving, ignoring the "Change Oil" light on your dashboard, but that would be bad for your engine. So, you get the oil changed and extend the life of your engine.

Or, how about this small choice:

In 2005, Facebook (a small, little-known startup company at that time) asked a graffiti artist named David Choe to paint their offices in Palo Alto, California. He had the choice to accept a few thousand dollars for his work, or he could take the same amount of money in the form of Facebook stock.

He took the stock.

Almost seven years later, when the company finally went public, Choe cashed in his stock for $200 million.[27]

DON'T TAKE THE EASY WAY

When it comes to your ministry, there are also choices that you make. Small, sometimes subtle choices that will either hold your ministry back or propel your ministry forward. What I've found is that the choices that hold your ministry back are usually the easy ones. I'm not saying that the choices are easy to make; I'm saying we take the easy way out when it's time to make these choices.

Maybe we don't want to be disruptive. Or maybe we don't have the energy to make the harder, better choice. Or maybe we don't have the influence required to change things. Whatever the reason, we often take the easy way. We make the easy choice, and the ministry remains stagnant as a result.

Nine times out of ten, if you took the harder way, did the harder thing, or made the harder choice, then your ministry would move forward in ways you can't even dream of right now.

What are these small choices that I'm talking about?

Let's take a look...

3 SMALL CHOICES THAT HOLD YOUR MINISTRY BACK

1. DO MINISTRY TOGETHER OR DO MINISTRY ALONE

You're probably expected to wear a lot of hats around your church. You prepare messages, plan services, choose songs, go to schools, recruit volunteers, attend meetings, and plenty more. If you try to do everything all by yourself, you will end up cheating both your ministry and yourself.

Your ministry will suffer because you can't be great at everything. You're a youth pastor, not a superhero! You have strengths and weaknesses. For the sake of quality, you need to work on your strengths and hand off your weaknesses to other people.

But that's not all. You also suffer personally when you do ministry alone because the definition of a weakness – according to Marcus Buckingham – is any activity that makes you feel "weak, bored, or drained."[28] Working alone in areas of weakness is a recipe for burnout. You have to stop.

Find ways to focus on your strengths and bring other people around you to help with everything else. Aggressively recruit those people because your future in ministry depends on it. Make the choice to do ministry together.

2. VALUE SKILLS OR VALUE FEELINGS

You probably have a small group leader who isn't doing a good job right now. Why don't you release that person of their duties? My guess is that you don't let that person go because either a) you don't have anyone who is willing to take their place or b) you're afraid to hurt their feelings.

You probably have a musician right now who isn't really good enough to be leading or playing on stage. They show up to play, but they haven't practiced. They don't know the words, so they stare at the music stand or the confidence monitor the whole time. And they think you don't notice. You know you need to have a conversation with that person, but you don't. Why not? Again, you're afraid of hurting their feelings.

Here's what you need to understand: Because you continue to avoid that hard conversation, your ministry is suffering.

When I was hired at one church, I discovered that we had a student praise band that played for our Wednesday night program. We also had an adult worship leader who was fairly young. Plus, he was pretty cool. The students liked him. He worked with the student praise band and prepared them to lead on Wednesday nights. However, the lead singer of the student band wasn't very good. He lacked the confidence to really sing and didn't know how to lead his peers. I understand that; it's tough to lead your peers. But we needed to do better than we were doing.

We didn't have enough money to pay another worship leader, so I had an idea: If the adult worship leader would lead for students on Wednesday nights, our program would be a lot better, and the students would be more engaged during the songs. Plus, the student worship leader could shadow him and learn a lot.

I called a meeting with the two of them (our adult worship leader and our student praise band worship leader). I explained that our music wasn't good enough. The program was designed to reach new students, but if we were actually going to attract anyone new, things had to be better. I suggested that adult worship leader leads on Wednesday nights, while the student played next to him and followed his lead.

Much to my surprise, there's wasn't any pushback at all. They both knew that my recommendation was better than what had been happening. We made the change, and our music quality went up tremendously.

Why hadn't the previous youth pastor made that change? I don't know, but it was a small choice that he made, and it held the ministry back. Make the choice to value skills.

3. Work In It or Work On It

Michael Gerber popularized this concept in his book, *The E-Myth Revisited*. The idea is that we often get caught up running the day-to-day, week-to-week parts of our ministries and don't think nearly enough about the strategies, systems, and structures that will take things to the next level in the future.

In other words, we tend to manage our ministries for today instead of leading them into tomorrow.

Working *in* it is easy because you just do what you've always done. There's no push. There's no disruption. There's no challenge. It's just maintaining the status quo.

Working *on* it is hard because it's exactly the opposite. You push. You disrupt. You challenge. You dream of new, innovative, different ways to accomplish your mission. When you work *on* your ministry, you constantly ask: "How can this be better?"

Working on my ministry has led me to things I never would've found otherwise. For example:

45

- When I wanted better curriculum, I discovered XP3.
- When I wanted to have good music playing before our services started, I discovered Spotify.
- When I wanted to make our games more fun, I discovered funninja.org.
- When I wanted to keep parents more informed, I discovered MailChimp.
- When I wanted to improve our graphics, I discovered a free online design program called Canva.
- When I wanted to engage on social media, I found apps like Font Candy.
- When I wanted a better way to train volunteers, I found training videos from Download Youth Ministry.

You get the point.

If I had just gone ahead with the way I had always done things, my ministry would've gotten stuck. You have to push forward and find new ways. Rise above the day-to-day and make the choice to work *on* your ministry.

YOUR MOVE

You can keep taking the easy way and holding your ministry back, or you can make the harder choices and propel your ministry forward. The choice is yours.

If you do ministry alone, you'll hold your ministry back. If you do ministry with others, you'll move your ministry forward.

If you value feelings, you'll hold your ministry back. If you value skills, you'll move your ministry forward.

If you work *in* it, you'll hold your ministry back. If you work *on* it, you'll move your ministry forward.

Which way will you choose?

STRATEGY #6:

Make the hard choices that will
move your ministry forward.

CHAPTER 7
HOW TO BUILD THE ULTIMATE MINISTRY BUDGET

If you're like most of the youth pastors I talk with, you dread budget season. You're convinced that Excel spreadsheets are *not* your friends. But here's the good news: You don't need to have a business degree to prepare a good youth ministry budget.

You just need to use a calendar and the categories I'm going to share with you, and you'll be on the fast-track to creating the ultimate youth ministry budget.

You didn't get into ministry to crunch numbers and track dollars and cents, but preparing a good budget will help you make the most of the resources you have.

BUDGETING 101

What is a budget? A budget is a spending plan. It allows you to predetermine when and how your ministry's money will be spent. It's often said that you can know what a person values by looking at how he spends his money. The same thing is true for a group. If you say you value something, make sure it's reflected in your budget.

You want to take a hard look at the budget to make sure you're getting as much return on investment as you can. This is much easier to do when the budget is divided into clear categories, with accurate estimates for how much money will be spent each month.

CONSIDER YOUR CATEGORIES

You should evaluate the budget at two levels:

1. Categories
2. Expenses

First, look at the categories in your budget.

I've seen ministry budgets that only list one lump sum of money to be spent during the year. That's not helpful for figuring out how much will be spent on what and when.

I've also seen ministry budgets that try to itemize every little thing. That's overkill, and it creates the need to constantly shift funds around to accommodate overspending on one thing and underspending on another.

Your youth ministry budget needs to have these ten categories:

1. ADMINISTRATION

Postage, pens, paper clips, and printing aren't free.

2. CURRICULUM & DISCIPLESHIP RESOURCES

You don't want to write everything yourself.

3. PRODUCTION SUPPLIES

This includes everything it takes to make a great program every week.

4. EVENTS

This includes camps, retreats, outings, mission trips, and special days.

5. ENVIRONMENT

You'll want to change up your space a few times to keep it fresh.

6. LEADER TRAINING & APPRECIATION

People who don't feel equipped and valued won't stick around.

7. MARKETING

Everyone loves a free t-shirt.

8. CARE

Sending birthday cards, eating with students, and showing up at games costs money.

9. HONORARIUMS

You need people to cover for you when you take a vacation.

10. PERSONAL DEVELOPMENT

Subscriptions, books, and training for yourself.

Are those categories in your current budget? If not, be sure to add them for next year.

ASSIGN DOLLAR AMOUNTS

Next, take out your calendar. You need to allocate dollar amounts to each of those categories and assign them to particular months throughout the year.

For instance, if you know you're going out of town for your brother's wedding in July, then put $100 from the Honorarium category for that month.

If you know that summer camp is in June, then list that money there. If you know that your curriculum subscription needs to be renewed in November, then add it.

It's a neat idea to recognize volunteers around Valentine's Day because you can say, "We LOVE our volunteers." Maybe give each of them a $10 gift card to Target. Tell them, "Thanks for helping us hit our target." If you want to do that, then put some of the Leader Training & Appreciation money in February.

I've seen youth pastors who spend all of their money before October and then scrape by in November and December. I've also seen guys who limit their capabilities all year long because they don't want to go over their budget, and then they blow the money at the end of the year on stuff they didn't really need because they have a use-it-or-lose-it mentality.

Assigning dollar amounts to each category for each

month will help you stay on track, so you don't overspend (or underspend) throughout the year.

Consider Your Expenses

Now, you're ready to dig into the specifics. Look at the actual expenses that have been charged to the budget for this year. I'll bet that you can find some opportunities for savings somewhere in there.

When I was hired at one church, I combed through the expense reports for the previous year. I noticed that we were paying $30 every month for a text messaging service. I got on the company's website and saw that we were subscribed to a plan that provided far more than what we actually needed. With the click of a button, I changed our plan and saved $20 per month.

Do the math:

$20 per month x 12 months = $240 per year.

That's real money that was being wasted every year!

Another area that the church was overspending was on curriculum. The publisher had two purchasing options. We could buy full-color, professionally printed student booklets for each series of lessons. Or we could buy a .pdf version of the same material with permission to make and distribute as many copies as we needed.

I inherited the first option.

But when the lessons were over, those booklets went straight in the trash. Even worse, half of the students either left their booklets at home or lost them before the sessions were over.

Because the program was aimed at educating Christian

students instead of reaching non-Christian students, I decided that it wasn't worth the extra money to get those booklets. We weren't trying to impress new students with flashy materials, so I didn't think there was a high enough return on investment to justify the cost. I made the switch to the .pdf version.

It saved us over $300.

With two simple changes, I had saved the church over $500 annually. That extra money allowed us to get donuts on Sunday mornings. Not just once a month, but every week. It was fully paid for by the money we had saved with those two simple changes.

The students never complained one time about not having those full-color booklets. Instead, they all raved about how awesome it was to get donuts every Sunday!

That's the benefit of having a good, thorough youth ministry budget.

YOUR MOVE

Every youth pastor wishes he had more money to use in his ministry. A good budget will help you make the most of the money you have.

In the Bonus Material for this book, I have included an Excel spreadsheet that is set up with the categories and formulas you need to set up a budget and track your actual expenses. It's the one that I use in my own ministry.

Budget season doesn't have to be the most stressful time of the year. If you prepare your budget properly, you'll have a spending plan that keeps you on track throughout the year.

STRATEGY #7:

Make the most of your dollars and cents.

CHAPTER 8
HOW TO FOCUS YOUR EFFORTS AND MAXIMIZE YOUR MINISTRY

Strategic initiatives are the best way to focus your efforts and maximize your ministry. If you're not familiar with strategic initiatives, think of them as short-term goals that move you closer to your long-term objectives. Strategic initiatives are at the end of the chain, down the line from your vision, mission, strategy, and objectives.

Picture the order like this:

Vision → Mission → Strategy → Objectives → Initiatives

AN EXAMPLE FROM MY CHURCH

Vision: Create a church that unchurched people love to attend.

Mission: Lead people into a growing relationship with Jesus Christ.

Strategy: Create environments where people are

encouraged and equipped to pursue intimacy with God, community with insiders, and influence with outsiders.

Objectives: Spiritual and Numerical Growth; Excellent and Irresistible Environments; Healthy Staff and Leadership Culture.

Initiatives: These are specific, measurable targets that will help us make significant progress toward each of our stated objectives.

Do you see how that works?

Again, the order is:

Vision → Mission → Strategy → Objectives → Initiatives

A Big Mistake

Many churches create vision and mission statements, but few actually drill down to the level of identifying initiatives. I think that's a big mistake.

Strategic initiatives help you focus on the things you need to focus on in a particular season of ministry. You might have fourteen things that need attention and improvement, but you can't get to everything all at once.

You have to decide which things will give you the highest return on investment over the next twelve months. Those are your strategic initiatives. They dictate where you need to spend the largest amounts of time, energy, and money to make the biggest difference. When you focus on those things and leave the other things for later, you will create positive momentum in your ministry.

As time passes, your initiatives will need to change to keep up with your current reality. They should evolve to account for new strengths, weaknesses, opportunities, threats, possibilities, and liabilities. Your initiatives shouldn't be the same from one year to the next.

Strategic initiatives help you accomplish great things, but they are also preventative. That is, they prevent Mission Drift.

What Is Mission Drift?

In their book, *Mission Drift: The Unspoken Crisis Facing Leaders, Charities, and Churches*, Peter Greer and Chris Horst explain, "Mission Drift unfolds slowly. Like a current, it carries organizations away from their core purpose and identity...[Unfortunately,] Mission Drift is the natural course for organizations, and it takes focused attention to safeguard against it."[29]

In science, the second law of thermodynamics says that in the natural order of the universe, things move toward chaos rather than progress. Your church and your ministry are the same way. The natural pull isn't toward alignment; the pull is toward misalignment.

In the average church, focus gets scattered. Resources get used. Things that should be priorities take a backseat to things that should've been done away with years ago.

Strategic initiatives help to keep your church and your ministry Mission True. Greer and Horst explain, "Mission True organizations know why they exist and protect their core at all costs. They remain faithful to what they believe God has entrusted them to do. They define what is immutable: their values and purposes, their DNA, their heart and soul."[30]

CLARIFYING QUESTIONS

Rather than share my church's strategic initiatives, I think it is more helpful to offer some questions that can help you clarify some of your own initiatives for your ministry.

When you're done answering these questions, you'll need to go back through them to define specific, measurable targets that are informed by your answers. Those will be your initiatives. I've also included a few examples that might be helpful for you to consider.

QUESTION 1:

What are we currently doing that hinders our ability to see more spiritual growth? How can we change that?

POSSIBLE INITIATIVE:

Find or create three serving opportunities within your church for students.

QUESTION 2:

What are two things we can do in the next twelve months to help students take a step in their relationship with God? How can we implement those?

POSSIBLE INITIATIVE:

Create a resource area for students that is stocked with resources to help them grow in their faith.

QUESTION 3:

What are we currently doing that hinders our ability to see

more new students attend and return to our programs? How can we change that?

POSSIBLE INITIATIVE:

Conduct a poll among parents to find the optimal program times.

QUESTION 4:

What are two things we can do in the next six months to attract new students to come and then come back? How can we implement those?

POSSIBLE INITIATIVE:

Implement a consistent follow-up system.

QUESTION 5:

What are two ways in which our student room hinders the experience we want students to have? How can we change that?

POSSIBLE INITIATIVE:

Find five parents who are willing to donate $500 each for room upgrades.

QUESTION 6:

What are two ways we can make our student room more appealing to students? How can we implement those?

POSSIBLE INITIATIVE:

Hire an interior designer to visit and give ideas.

QUESTION 7:

What keeps new volunteers from joining the team? How can we change that?

POSSIBLE INITIATIVE:

Create an entry-level serving position that doesn't require very much time, training, or commitment.

QUESTION 8:

What are two ways we can create a greater sense of unity among our volunteers? How can we implement those?

POSSIBLE INITIATIVE:

Host a cookout for volunteers at your house.

QUESTION 9:

What keeps you from consistently updating your ministry's social media? How can you change that?

POSSIBLE INITIATIVE:

Create a social media calendar to plan your posts in advance.

QUESTION 10:

What keeps you from growing as a leader? How can you change that?

POSSIBLE INITIATIVE:

Read three leadership books in the next six months.

YOUR MOVE

Stating your initiatives isn't enough. It's a good start, but there's more to it than that. They won't happen without corresponding action steps. That's why I included the secondary questions about "how?"

For example, if you're going to host a cookout for volunteers at your house, there are several more steps involved. You have to pick a date, make sure you have money in the budget, buy the supplies, get things ready, and plan for the time together.

The initiative gets the ball rolling, but don't forget to define your action steps. It's those action steps that will help you accomplish your initiatives.

When you accomplish your initiatives, you'll meet your objectives. When you meet your objectives, you'll be in sync with your strategy. When you're in sync with your strategy, you'll accomplish your mission. And when you accomplish your mission, you'll make progress toward your vision. It all works together, but the real progress happens when you identify your strategic initiatives and take steps toward achieving them.

STRATEGY #8:

Identify and achieve your strategic initiatives.

CHAPTER 9
WHY VISION SLIPS
(AND HOW TO MAKE IT STICK)

Vision is important for your ministry. George Barna says, "Ministry without vision is like a car without gasoline: capable of forward movement, but lacking the necessary fuel."[31] Your ministry is capable of moving forward, but if volunteers, students, and parents don't understand and embrace your vision, then you won't go anywhere.

Your vision is a clear mental picture of a preferred future. It is sparked by your passion. It gives you motivation. It clarifies your direction. It provides you with purpose. Your vision is an important part of your ministry.

Unfortunately, the problem with vision is that it leaks. It slips. When you cast your vision, people buy into it. But then they forget about it. They get on with their other responsibilities, with their own jobs and kids.

Rick Warren calls this the "Nehemiah Principle." He says, "Vision and purpose have to be restated every twenty-six days to keep the church moving in the right direction."[32]

WHY DOES VISION SLIP?

In his book, *Visioneering*, Andy Stanley observes, "The daily grind of life is hard on visions. Life is now. Bills are now. Crisis is now. Vision is later…Distractions can slowly kill a vision."[33]

Distractions usually come in three forms:

1. OPPORTUNITIES

All sorts of things will come up that can take your attention away from what God has called you to do. Entertainment, vacation, relationships, and business opportunities are a few that come to mind. Most of the opportunities that come your way won't necessarily be bad opportunities. They'll probably be good. You could easily justify them if you wanted to. But those are the things that will keep you from the one thing God has really called you to do.

Stanley says, "To accomplish the important things you must learn to say no to some good things."[34]

2. CRITICISM

When you are focused on one vision, when you operate with a singular devotion, you will most likely become a target of criticism. People won't be accustomed to that kind of focus and intensity. They won't know how to respond. They'll try to cover their own lack of care and concern by criticizing your abundance of care and concern.

Stanley points out, "There are always going to be accusations when you are focused on accomplishing a vision. Men and women with vision stand out. That makes people uncomfortable. The current society always moves in the direction of conformity."[35]

3. FEAR

Vision sees a future that isn't a reality yet. It's unknown. That gap can create a real sense of fear in some people. It's easy to imagine the bad things that might happen rather than the good things that God desires.

Stanley counsels, "Don't allow the fear of the unknown to cause you to miss out on what God wants to do through you...Don't allow fear to distract you from what you believe could and should be."[36]

With these potential distractions, making vision stick can be difficult. But it *is* possible.

HOW TO MAKE VISION STICK

In his little book, *Making Vision Stick,* Andy Stanley offers five things you can do to significantly increase the stick-iness of your vision.

1. STATE THE VISION SIMPLY

"If your vision is going to stick in people's minds, it must be memorable."[37]

2. CAST THE VISION CONVINCINGLY

"Once you have your vision in a form that makes it easy to communicate, you must communicate it in a way that moves people to action."[38]

3. Repeat the Vision Regularly

"We all need to be reminded why we are doing what we are doing. We need to be reminded what's at stake. We need to be reminded of the vision. And we need it more often than most leaders realize."[39]

4. Celebrate the Vision Systematically

"To make vision stick, a leader needs to pause long enough to celebrate the wins along the way. Celebrating the wins does more to clarify the vision than anything else."[40]

5. Embrace the Vision Personally

"Living out the vision establishes credibility and makes you a leader worth following. When people are convinced that the vision has stuck with you, it is easier for them to make the effort to stick with the vision."[41]

Your Move

Both you and your team need a significant vision to keep going for the long haul. If you're short-sighted, then you'll throw in the towel.

It's easy to become distracted by the tyranny of the urgent. Opportunities, criticism, and fear get in the way and cloud our judgment. Vision must be stated simply, cast convincingly, repeated regularly, celebrated systematically, and embraced personally in order to become a reality.

It's not complicated, but it *is* hard. Stay focused. Work hard. And your ministry will eventually see the results that come from dreaming big.

STRATEGY #9:

Help people see, experience, and remember your vision.

CHAPTER 10
WHAT DO YOUR VOLUNTEERS REALLY WANT?

Nick Marshall was a successful advertising executive in Chicago when his life took a strange twist. He was great at marketing to men but didn't understand women at all. Because his company recognized their need to expand their appeal to women, they decided to hire someone else – a woman – for the position Marshall wanted. That didn't sit well with him.

He wanted to prove himself as capable of appealing to women, so he had an idea: he would try out several women's beauty products and then try to write some advertisements from a woman's perspective. That night, while holding an electric hairdryer, he fell into the bathtub and shocked himself. When he regained his consciousness, he noticed something different.

He could hear voices. But they weren't just any voices. They were the voices inside women's heads. He had gained the ability to hear what women were actually thinking. With that knowledge, he became a marketing superstar because he knew exactly what women wanted.

In case you're wondering, that's not a true story. It's the plot from a movie called *What Women Want*, which came out in 2000 and starred Mel Gibson in the role of Nick Marshall. Even so, it's a good idea. If you can figure out what your volunteers want, you will have a greater chance of giving it to them.

So, here's what I want you to do:

Think back to the days when you weren't on staff at a church. Remember back when you were a volunteer. For some of you, that's a long trip down memory lane. For others, it's a bit shorter. Either way, if you're working in full-time ministry now, I'm guessing you were a volunteer somewhere along the way.

I want you to think back to those days because I want you to remember what *you* wanted as a volunteer.

What made *you* say yes?

What made *you* show up week after week?

What made *you* feel like you were making a difference?

Understanding what *you* wanted as a volunteer will help you understand what your volunteers want. And understanding what your volunteers really want will help you lead them better.

When I think about what I wanted as a volunteer, seven things stand out.

7 THINGS YOUR VOLUNTEERS REALLY WANT

1. FUN

Your volunteers want to have a good time. They want to laugh. They want to enjoy what they're doing. Life is too short to waste time with things that are boring and lame. Volunteering should feel more like fun and less like work.

ACTION STEP: Look for ways to add levity and laughter to your ministry.

2. TEAM

Your volunteers want to feel like they're part of a movement. They want to be on a team that's shaking things up and reaching students for Christ. Volunteering is a great way for someone to meet new people and feel connected to your church. That sense of team is the reason why some of your volunteers stick around year after year.

ACTION STEP: Make sure your volunteers know each other's names and stories.

3. SPIRITUAL GROWTH

Your volunteers want to grow in their relationship with Christ. They've said yes to an opportunity to grow in their own faith while contributing to the faith of others. Andy Stanley is right when he says, "Ministry makes people's faith bigger."[42] As they prepare, learn, and lead, your volunteers are walking with God in a way that is not accessible to people who don't volunteer. Maybe that's what keeps them coming back.

ACTION STEP: Give your volunteers opportunities to stretch their faith.

4. Sense of Purpose

Your volunteers want to feel like they're making a difference. They have a sense that they were made for more than a life spent commuting to and from an office or staying at home all day. Binge watching shows on Netflix isn't nearly as satisfying as the advertisements make it seem. Your volunteers crave a sense of purpose. Serving can give it to them.

Action Step: Tell your volunteers about the difference they're making in students' lives.

5. Care

Your volunteers want to know that you care about them, not just their performance. Recently, I visited two of my volunteers in their homes. One has breast cancer. The other had a knee replacement. Those visits are important because they communicate my care for those people beyond what they're able to produce in our ministry. When you care for volunteers, they will care for students.

Action Step: Let your volunteers know how much you value them.

6. Consistency

Your volunteers want to know what they can expect from you. They have their own lives and families to keep up with, so you need to do what you can to eliminate the guesswork for them. Send the lessons out on the same day every week. Hold your meetings on a regularly scheduled date. Don't change things over and over again. Make a decision and stick with it. Don't be super-positive one week and super-negative the next. Do what you say you'll do. Be consistent.

ACTION STEP: Create a schedule and stick to it.

7. NEW OPPORTUNITIES

Your volunteers want the chance to advance. Be willing to hand off more responsibility to your high-capacity volunteers. When you were fourteen years old, it was exciting to drive your parents' car around the cul-de-sac. When you were sixteen, you wanted to take that car out of the neighborhood. Leaders want to feel like they're making progress. If they don't, they'll find something else to do. Increased responsibility is a sign of increased trust.

ACTION STEP: Identify one of your volunteers who is ready for more responsibility.

YOUR MOVE

Take some time to remember what it was like when you were a volunteer.

What made you say yes?

What made you show up week after week?

What made you feel like you were making a difference?

Make a list of the things you wanted. When you're done, I think your list will probably look a lot like mine. But don't stop with making a list. To make a difference you have to take action. Make a plan for how you will help your volunteers experience the things they really want.

STRATEGY #10:

Give your volunteers what they really want.

CHAPTER 11
HOW TO BUILD A HIGH-PERFORMANCE VOLUNTEER TEAM

Some of our friends had a get-together recently. They had just finished a big project in their backyard, so they were excited to show it off. The email invitation said, "Come over for a relaxed night of outdoor fun. We'll have Taco Soup, play games, eat s'mores, and hang out by the new fire pit."

And that's exactly what we did. It was a fun night.

A few weeks later, my wife and I invited some of our other friends to our house for dinner. When I started thinking about what we would eat, my mind went back to the Taco Soup we had eaten at the backyard party a few weeks before. It was delicious! So, I decided that I would make Taco Soup.

There was just one problem:

I didn't have the recipe.

But it didn't seem like a big problem. How hard could it be? I knew what most of the ingredients were: ground beef, tomatoes, taco seasoning, and water. Put it all in a pot and let it simmer, right?

Wrong.

Because I tried to make it without the recipe, my version of Taco Soup was nothing like what our friends had served us. It was actually pretty disgusting. So, we ordered pizza instead.

The next day, I did what I should have done in the first place: I called our friends and asked for the Taco Soup recipe. The next time I made it, I followed the recipe and it tasted exactly like it was supposed to taste, delicious.

Following the recipe made all the difference.

By the way, I've included that recipe for Taco Soup in the Bonus Material for this book. I think you're going to love it!

A RECIPE FOR BUILDING TEAMS

Mark Miller, Vice President for Organizational Effectiveness at Chick-fil-A, has shared the company's secret recipe for building high-performance teams.

And here's the good news: It's probably not as complicated as you think it is, especially when you know the right ingredients.

Miller says, "High-performance teams focus on talent, skills, and community."[43] That's it. It's not complicated.

Talent.

Skills.

Community.

If you're going to grow your team of volunteers, then you should focus on recruiting talented people, helping them develop the skills they need, and building a community in which they know and care for each other.

HOW TO DO IT

1. RECRUIT TALENTED PEOPLE

Hold the bar high. You want people on your team who want to be around students. Sometimes you meet people who you just know would be a good fit on the team. They have an "it" quality that would really resonate with students. Recruit those people.

Don't rely on bulletin updates or announcements made from the stage. Go after the people you think could help your ministry thrive. Often times, they're just waiting to be asked.

Here's a pitch that I've used lots of times with great success:

"I think you'd be great at working with students. They would love you! Would you be interested in meeting for lunch one day to talk about what that might look like?"

That line has scored me dozens of high-quality volunteers who weren't already serving anywhere else in the church.

2. DEVELOP THEIR SKILLS

To begin with, every volunteer should be clear about their role and their goal. They should be able to answer these two questions:

What am I supposed to be doing? (role)

What does success look like? (goal)

Beyond those two questions, you want to make sure your volunteers have the tools necessary to do what you're asking them to do. A few years ago, the Gallup Organization had its researchers look through over 1 million employee interviews from previous decades to find out what drives employee satisfaction and engagement. Twelve things stood out, but having the right tools topped the list. Here's what they found:

"Of the 12 Elements, whether a person has the materials and equipment needed to do his work well is the strongest indicator of job stress. The data show there are few things more frustrating than to want to make a difference at work, and then to be held back by inadequate resources."[44]

Don't frustrate your volunteers. Give them the roles, goals, tools, and training that they need in order to do a good job.

3. BUILD A COMMUNITY

At the end of the day, we all just want to do good work with good people and have a good time together. Think about how you can create shared memories with your volunteer team.

You could:

- Do a cookout at your house. It doesn't have to be expensive. Tell everyone to bring their own meat, and you'll grill it.
- Meet for a night of bowling. Make up crazy nicknames for each other to post on the scoreboard.
- Send birthday cards.
- Ask about their kids.

Get to know your volunteers and let them get to know

you. I remember two couples that were on my team. They didn't know each other before they started working with students, but they met and hit it off. Pretty soon they had lined up a double date to get dinner and see a movie. They became close friends, and they're still committed volunteers today.

Think of creative ways to show appreciation too. You have to keep in mind that people have their own jobs and their own lives. There are a lot of other places they could be and a lot of other things they could be doing. But they're there. With you. Volunteering. Show them some appreciation.

You could:

- Give them a gift card to Starbucks.
- Send them their favorite candy, just because.
- Take a student over to their house and wash their car.
- Feature them as the volunteer of the month on social media.

Whatever it takes, let them know that you value them.

YOUR MOVE

To make the biggest difference with students, you need to surround yourself with high-caliber volunteers who are consistently involved.

Recruit them.

Develop them.

Appreciate them.

Those personal touches will help you build a high-performance volunteer team that makes doing youth ministry a lot more fun and a lot more effective.

STRATEGY #11:

Build a high-performance volunteer team.

CHAPTER 12
WHAT YOUR SMALL GROUP LEADERS SHOULD BE DOING

The boys' basketball team from Hugo High School was on their way to the next round of the 2013 Oklahoma state playoffs. There were only 2.9 seconds left in the game, and they led the team from Millwood High School by one point: 37 to 36.

Even better, Hugo had possession of the ball. A quick inbound pass, a few dribbles, and the buzzer would sound. The game would be over. Cheerleaders would cheer, and the teams would shake hands and head to the locker room.

Trey Johnson, a junior at Hugo, received the pass. What he did next shocked everyone in the gym.

Instead of dribbling until the buzzer sounded, he saw an opening on the court. He sprinted past the defenders until he was staring at an open goal. He took the shot. And he made it.

There was just one problem: he scored that shot in his own basket.[45]

That shot gave Millwood the victory: 38 to 37.

That's too bad for Trey Johnson. He scored the goal, but he scored it in the wrong basket. But here's a question for you: How many of your small group leaders are shooting at the wrong basket every week?

You know who they are.

They think their role is to show up and get through the lesson you provide. They think their goal is to end on time and make sure no one breaks any of the furniture in the room. And as long as they show up, get through the lesson, end on time, and make sure nothing gets broken, they feel like they're doing a good job.

But they're not. That's the wrong goal.

The goal for your small group leaders is so much bigger and more important than those things. You owe it to them to clarify the win. They need you to tell them which basket they should shoot at.

Once you've told them, you need to keep telling them. Remember? Vision leaks. It slips. So, you have to keep showing and telling your small group leaders what their goals really are.

So, what are their goals?

5 GOALS FOR SMALL GROUP LEADERS

If a leader wants to help their students get the most out of their small group experience, these five things must be happening:

1. STAY CONNECTED

Leading a small group requires the leader to pour out for

students what God is pouring into him or her. That means the small group leader must have a consistent, vibrant relationship with God.

They must stay connected to the Source of Life if they want to be able to lead others in that direction. This is not negotiable. That's why Jesus said, "I am the vine; you are the branches. Those who remain in me, and I in them will produce much fruit" (John 15:5 NLT).

When your leaders stay connected to Jesus, their efforts with students will produce fruit. If you have a leader who complains about students and has a bad attitude about everything you do, it's a good bet that he or she isn't staying connected to Jesus.

A leader's connection with Jesus is the foundation for their connection with students.

2. Build Relationships

The biggest problems in small groups happen when the leader thinks he can just show up, teach, go home, and do it again next week. But that's not how it works. That creates problems because those students won't listen to that person. Eventually, that person will get frustrated, blame the students, and quit.

Students want to know that the leader actually likes them. Beyond that, they don't care what the leader knows until they know that the leader cares. It's only after students are convinced that their leader likes them and cares about them that will they listen and engage at a deeper level in their group.

This shouldn't be hard to understand. Think about any meaningful relationships you have. The hallmark of those relationships is transparency. You feel free to say what you really think and show how you really feel. But transparency doesn't happen overnight. It's a by-product of trust that is built over time. That's what you want for your students, and that's what your students want from their small group leaders.

If a small group leader doesn't make relationships a priority, they have a frustrating road ahead of them.

3. Encourage Participation

Too many small group leaders talk too much. That's a problem because small groups are intended to get the *students* talking. Instead of talking, your small group leaders should be playing a different kind of game. They should try to see how little they can talk. When they don't fill the air with their own voices, it leaves room for students to talk.

This usually requires a shift in the leader's view of their role. They are not *teachers of information*. They are *facilitators of discussion*. Their goal isn't to get through all of the material. Their goal is to get everyone to participate in a meaningful way.

That means they can't let the same three students answer all the questions and dominate the discussion. They must be willing to call on a quiet student by name and ask, "What do you think about that, Alex?"

When group leaders get group members to participate, the group will grow together.

4. Provide Care

Care is needed when a student stumbles into a challenging time in their life. Sometimes it's their own fault: they cheated on a test, went too far with their boyfriend, or said the wrong thing at the wrong time to the wrong person. Other times, it's not their fault: a grandparent dies, their parents get divorced, or a girlfriend breaks up with them.

Whatever the case, when students hit hard times they look to the people they know. They talk to the people they trust. God uses pivotal circumstances to grow a person's faith, but it doesn't happen automatically. A pivotal circumstance has the potential to either strengthen or weaken a student's faith. Which way they go can depend on the quality of care they receive in the midst of the challenge they're facing. They need small group leaders to help them see God's goodness in the midst of life's challenges.

Because they've earned the right to be heard when times were good, small group leaders are able to provide care when times aren't so good.

5. Focus on Life Change

Isn't this the point of everything your church and ministry do? And yet, life change easily slips into the background. It drifts out of focus.

Too often, our small group leaders become preoccupied with planning outings or minimizing behavior problems. Those things need to be done, but those things aren't the reason the small group exists. Life change is the ultimate goal of the group. The reason your ministry has small groups in the first place is to create an environment where God is able to work in the lives of students. The relationships, discussion, and care are all pointing in this direction.

Leaders who focus on life change are the leaders who eventually see life change happen in their group. Why?

Because they're praying about it, talking about it, and planning for it.

In his book, *The Soul Winner,* Charles Spurgeon writes about a conversation he had with a new minister. The minister tells Spurgeon that he's been preaching for several months, but still hasn't seen a single convert to the faith.

What was Spurgeon's reply?

He said, "And do you expect that the Lord is going to bless you and save souls every time you open your mouth?

"No sir," the new minister replied.

"Well then that is why you do not get souls saved," Spurgeon told him.

Group leaders can't by shy about expecting and encouraging students to take next steps in their relationship with Christ. Maybe that's salvation. Maybe that's baptism. Maybe that's repentance. Maybe that's surrender. Whatever it is, life change must remain the primary focus of the small group leader and the ultimate goal of the group.

YOUR MOVE

Don't let your small group leaders shoot at the wrong basket. They are showing up, trying to make a difference. But they need you to keep the right goals in front of them week after week.

Again, the goals are:

- Stay connected.
- Build relationships.
- Encourage participation.

- Provide care.
- Focus on life change.

Small groups matter because they enable students to take steps toward God, and that can change their lives both today and forever.

In the Bonus Material, I have included these goals in a one-page document that you can print and give to your small group leaders. Tell them that you want to make sure everyone knows what they're supposed to be doing because the strength and quality of your ministry is directly affected by the strength and quality of your groups.

STRATEGY #12:

Clarify the win for your small group leaders.

CHAPTER 13
HOW TO GET YOUR VOLUNTEERS MORE INVOLVED

Don't you hate it? You try to get your adult volunteers to jump in and sit with the students, but they just stand against the back wall. It's like the wall has Velcro on it, and they can't break free.

Why do they do that?

I think a lot of them do that because that's how they saw youth ministry modeled when they were younger. Students would be together in the front of the room, while adults talked amongst themselves in the back of the room.

It seemed to work. After all, they're there, aren't they?

So, they're doing what they think they should be doing.

Other volunteers might just be uncomfortable. They are self-conscious, so they feel like the students will think less of them for joining in with them. They think it'll look like they're trying too hard to fit in. But you and I know that's not the case. When an adult volunteer jumps into the action, it actually has the opposite effect. But they don't know that.

Here's one of the biggest reasons why they're standing on the back wall instead of joining in with the students:

New volunteers take their cues from existing volunteers.

When a new person shows up to serve in your ministry, they learn quickly. If the volunteers who have been with you for a while are standing against the back wall during your program, where do you think the new volunteer will go?

Yep. They're heading straight to the back wall.

How can you change that?

5 WAYS TO GET YOUR VOLUNTEERS MORE INVOLVED

1. TELL THEM WHY

Simon Sinek has the third most popular TED Talk of all time. It's called, "How Great Leaders Inspire Action." Sinek says, "When most organizations or people think, act, or communicate they do so from the outside in, from WHAT to WHY…We say WHAT we do, we sometimes say HOW we do it, but we rarely say WHY we do what we do. But not the inspired companies. Not the inspired leaders. Every single one of them, regardless of their size or their industry, thinks, acts and communicates from the inside out."[46]

In other words, great leaders start with why.

Clearly, what he's saying has struck a chord with many viewers and readers. It seems that people know what they're supposed to do, but they don't know the bigger purpose of why they're supposed to be doing it. And when they don't know the why, they slack on the what.

If you want your volunteers to get off the back wall, then you have to tell them why. If you want your volunteers to jump in and mingle with students, then tell them why it matters. Tell them why it makes a difference.

One of the easiest ways to do this is to say something like:

"We believe our message has the power to change students' lives, so we want to create a place they want to come to. Of course, we can't compete with every other entertainment option they have. We do our best every week to make our program as appealing as it can be, but we recognize our limits. However, there's one thing we can do better than anyone else: love students.

We can create a place where they know they're known and cared about. That doesn't happen when you're over here and they're over there. It happens when you talk with students as they show up, sit with them during the program, and follow-up with them when it's over.

When that happens week after week, you'll gain credibility with the students, and this will be a place they can't resist!"

If someone doesn't get inspired by hearing that, then they might not be a good fit for youth ministry.

2. Give Them Specific Instructions

Andy Stanley says, "Without clear direction, [volunteers] are forced to chart their own course or follow whoever has the best plan at the moment."[47] Don't assume your volunteers know what they should do. They probably don't.

My volunteers range from business executives to stay-at-home moms. But when it comes to my ministry, I'm the expert. They look to me for instructions about what they should be doing. If I don't give them specific instructions, then it's my fault when they don't do what I want them to do.

Like I said in the previous chapter, every volunteer needs a role and a goal. If you have a volunteer on your Host Team, give them a specific role and a specific goal. Tell them: "You're going to be at the front door today. I want you to greet every student with a big smile and a high-five. Tell them it's an awesome day to be here. And, while you're at it, try to learn three students' names that you didn't know before today."

If you have someone working in the snack area, their role could be: keep this area clean and stocked with food. Their goal could be to ask three students which snack is their favorite.

I had a volunteer who asked that question, wrote down the students' answers, and then gave them their favorite snack on their birthday. I didn't ask her to do that; she went above and beyond the call. But it started with specific instructions. She had a role and a goal, even in the snack area.

If you have volunteers who are standing against the back wall during your program, they might see their role as "chaperone" and their goal as "keep students from getting too rowdy." If that's the case, then your role is "leader," and your goal is to change that.

It might be as simple as giving them specific instructions for what to do and where to sit during the program.

3. Highlight Positive Examples

Highlighters are useful when you're reading a book. When you come across something you want to recall later, you highlight it to make it stand out from the other sentences on the page. Then, the next time you pick up that book again, your eyes will naturally gravitate toward those things you highlighted.

The same thing happens for your volunteers. If you want to reinforce the right actions, then highlight people who are doing those actions well. Call attention to them. Celebrate them.

Andy Stanley says, "Here's an organizational principle you don't want to lose sight of: What's celebrated is repeated. The behaviors that are celebrated are repeated. The decisions that are celebrated are repeated. The values that are celebrated are repeated...Celebrations trump motivational speeches every time."[48]

This should happen both privately and publicly. When you catch someone doing something right, let them know it. The sooner, the better.

When a small group leader handles a situation with a disruptive student, you could say, "The way you handled that situation was great! I don't know if I could've done it as well as you just did."

When one of your volunteers moves off the back wall and sits with students for the first time, send them a text message on the way home to say, "Hey, I loved seeing you in there with the students today! Even better, I know they loved having you in there with them. You're making a difference!"

Those private celebrations are good, but you also want to share those success stories with your other volunteers.

One simple way to do that is by sending out an email on the day after your program. Make the subject line: "Wins from Yesterday." You could include the following:

- number of students who attended
- number of first-time attenders
- names of students who brought friends
- any spiritual decisions that were made

All of these things are good to pass along to volunteers because it helps them see that your ministry is moving forward and accomplishing great things.

You should also include a story about a volunteer who did something good. You could say something like:

"Big shout out to Rick! I saw him talking to a group of 7th grade guys last night. They were all cracking up. I don't know what they were talking about, but I know Rich left a big impression on them. One guy's mom already emailed me this morning to say how much her son enjoyed being at church yesterday. Great job, Rich!"

There are all sorts of ways to celebrate your volunteers. For example, you could post a picture of a volunteer on social media with a story about what they did. Or, the next time you have a chance to preach to the whole congregation, your sermon could include stories of volunteers who are doing it right and making a difference. Be creative with your celebrations.

When you highlight positive examples like that, you'll see them happening more often. Be on the lookout for ways your volunteers are doing a good job. When you see it, celebrate them both privately and publicly.

4. SEND REMINDERS

Even if you've taken the time to clarify your expectations during the volunteer orientation process, most of your volunteers forget. Remember: You think about this stuff all the time. You hang around students. You visit school campuses. You're comfortable in the environment because it's your natural habitat.

The same isn't true for your volunteers. They think about their own lives all week. They spend most of their time around other adults. Engaging with students probably isn't natural to them (even for parents).

That's why it's so important to communicate your expectations and specific instructions every week. If you want your volunteers to sit with students, tell them. If you want your volunteers to sing when the band plays, tell them. If you want your volunteers to show up early or stay late, tell them. If you want your volunteers to get off the back wall, tell them.

5. INCLUDE THEM IN GAMES

One way to help your volunteers feel more comfortable around students is to get them up on the stage for a game. This is actually a shift that I've seen happen over the last ten years of youth ministry.

When I started out, I never would've thought to include volunteers in games. I assumed games were just for the students. It's not that way now. I try to include volunteers in games a few times every month. You could team them up with a student to compete against another volunteer and student in a Minute to Win It challenge. Or maybe you could pair them up with another volunteer to compete against a pair of students in a trivia game.

I would even encourage you to let your volunteers get messy. In the past, students wanted to be part of messy games. They were willing to put shaving cream all over their faces and have cheese balls thrown at them. Today, most students don't want to do that. But they love to see volunteers do it!

An easy way to do this is to bring a couple of volunteers on stage to play the Pie Face! game from Hasbro. Our students love it, and the volunteers have fun too.

Games are an easy, non-threatening, light-hearted way to get your volunteers more involved.

Your Move

If you want to get your volunteers to stop standing on the back wall and start jumping in with your students, pick one of these ideas to do this week:

- Tell them why.
- Give them specific instructions.
- Highlight positive examples.
- Send reminders.
- Include them in games.

STRATEGY #13:

Do everything you can to
get your volunteers more involved.

CHAPTER 14
WHAT SHOULD YOU HAND OFF TO VOLUNTEERS?

To be effective in youth ministry over the long haul, you can't do everything by yourself. You need people around you to share the load. That realization was a big turning point for me. Trying to do everything myself led me to the brink of burnout.

In the aftermath, I experienced what Andrew Carnegie observed in the latter part of his life when he said, "It marks a big step in your development when you come to realize that other people can help you do a better job than you can do alone."

You've probably figured that out by now. You know you need help. You know you need volunteers.

If you're like me, two questions come to mind when you realize you can't do everything by yourself:

1. What are the things I should keep doing?

2. What are the things I should hand off?

To answer those questions, you'll need to think about how your strengths intersect with the goals of your church and needs of your ministry.

CONSIDER YOUR STRENGTHS

In his book, *The Next Generation Leader*, Andy Stanley tells about his struggles when he started out as a youth pastor. He arrived at the office early and went home late. He was always on the go. But he realized that he wasn't working smart. He remembers, "The majority of my time was devoted to tasks I was not good at. I was eight years into my career before I realized that my real value to our organization lay within the context of my giftedness, not the number of hours I worked."[49]

Did you catch that?

His real value was when he worked *within the context of his giftedness.* The same thing is true for you: Your gifts are a gift to your ministry.

God has gifted you in unique ways. He has connected you with your particular church at this particular time. The worst thing you can do, then, is to withhold your gifts from your ministry because you're too busy doing things that are outside of your giftedness. You add the most value to your ministry when you focus on the two or three areas where you're most gifted.

What Andy Stanley calls "gifts," Marcus Buckingham calls "strengths."

When Buckingham worked for the Gallup Organization, he discovered some key themes when successful leaders were interviewed about excellence and peak performance. In particular, he found that strengths are made up of three separate components:

1. TALENTS

Talents are personality traits that you're born with. They don't change very much during your life, but they influence everything about the way you think and act.

2. SKILLS

Skills are abilities that are developed through trial and error. They help you perform specific tasks and duties in every aspect of your life.

3. KNOWLEDGE

Knowledge is an understanding that is discovered through instruction and observation. It helps you make sense of yourself and your environment.

Buckingham summarizes, "Your strengths are those activities that make you feel strong. (The flip side is also true: 'An activity that makes you feel weak' is the best definition of a weakness.)"[50]

Whether you call it a strength or a gift, you need to focus on the few areas where you're strongest if you want to make the biggest impact in your ministry.

How can you do that?

Let's go back to Andy Stanley. After realizing that his real value was in the context of his giftedness, he says, "I began looking for ways to redefine my job description according to what I was good at, rather than what I was willing to do."[51]

CONSIDER YOUR JOB DESCRIPTION

You probably haven't looked at your job description since

the day you were hired, but take a minute to track it down and read it. If you can't find one, I've included an example for you in the Bonus Material.

Consider these questions as you're reading:

- What are the things that make you feel energized?
- What are the things that make you feel depleted?
- Which tasks do you most enjoy in your current role?
- What do you wish you could hand off to someone else?
- Which of your gifts or strengths are not currently being utilized to the fullest?
- What do you do that is almost effortless from your perspective but seems challenging to others?
- In what areas do people consider you the "go-to" person?
- What do you do that brings the most praise and recognition from others?
- What situations do you look forward to working in?
- What situations do you avoid?
- If you could focus more of your time and attention on only one or two things in your job, what would they be?

Your goal is to rearrange and reprioritize your schedule around your strengths. You might think that you can't redefine your job description, but you can. You just have to understand the church's goals for your ministry before you change anything.

Ask yourself, or ask your pastor:

Why did they hire you?

What did they hire you to do?

What results do they expect you to produce?

As long as you're making progress on the things for which you were hired, you'll be fine.

By the way, I'm not talking about making a formal change to your job description. Depending on the kind of church you're in, that could require a bulletin announcement, a committee meeting, and congregational vote. All of that is unnecessary for the change that I'm talking about. The point here is to figure out how to accomplish the job you were hired to do while also leveraging your strengths as much as you can.

ONLY DO WHAT ONLY YOU CAN DO

Let's go back to those two questions that we started with:

1. What are the things I should keep doing?

2. What are the things I should hand off?

Here are my answers:

What are the things you should keep doing? Your goal should be to only do what only you can do.

What are the things you should hand off? Everything else.

This is important to understand: Your willingness to do everything doesn't make you more valuable to your ministry. Instead, you must realize that you are most valuable to your ministry when you limit your focus to your areas of strength. That happens when you decide to only do what only you can do.

This one change will do more to accelerate your ministry than anything else you can do as a leader.

YOUR MOVE

Discovering your strengths forces you to identify the activities that bring out the best you have to offer. That's your sweet spot. Those are the things you need to focus on. They are the things that will bring the greatest return on investment for your time and effort.

This week, use the time audit tool included in the Bonus Material to track how you're spending your time. You only get 168 hours each week. You will be more satisfied personally and more valuable to your ministry when you're using your strengths for most of that time.

You might be wondering, "But what about everything else?" Well, that's what volunteers are for.

STRATEGY #14:

Organize your schedule around your strengths.

CHAPTER 15

REACHING MORE STUDENTS BY DOING FEWER THINGS

A few years ago, I was working at a traditional church. The structure I inherited included an off-site activity every Sunday night after the service. Participation was limited to pretty much the same fifteen students every week. That was okay. After all, having those students involved was better than losing them.

But the program lacked vitality and energy. No one looked forward to it. They did it just because they were accustomed to doing it.

For me, it was a time-hog. It required lots of planning and promotion to put those off-site activities together and communicate all the details for them every week. It was a lot of work with very little return on investment. It's for that reason that Andy Stanley says, "You have to do less if you want to grow more. And if you do more, chances are you will grow less."[52]

I decided to redesign it. We moved from doing an activity every Sunday night to doing an activity only on the final

Sunday of the month. Instead of doing fifty-two random activities throughout the year, we would only do twelve attractive events.

There were several advantages to this change:

1. It coincided with our student-led worship night, which was also on the final Sunday night of the month.

2. One of the factors that limited our attendance was the time slot. It was dinner time, and students were hungry. By hosting only twelve events, we had the money available to provide pizza and drinks for everyone who attended. When we were doing fifty-two activities, the budget wasn't big enough to do that.

3. By getting together less frequently, we actually increased the value of the times when we got together. This is a basic principle of supply and demand.

4. There were fewer details to communicate, so I was able to spend several weeks getting the word out before the events. That led to increased participation simply because people had more awareness of what was going on.

WHAT WERE THE RESULTS?

The change immediately yielded positive results:

Participation went up.

Enthusiasm went up.

It wasn't long before a dad showed up to pick up his son after one of our Sunday night events. The place was packed, and everyone was having a good time. The dad made a comment that seemed to make sense. He said, "It's a shame you guys don't do this every week. That would really be great."

It would be easy to get sucked into his line of reasoning. What we were doing seemed to be working. Why not do it more often? Why not do it every week?

The fact is that we *had* tried doing it every week. Nobody came, including his son. And the only reason that this dad was there to see the good things that were happening on that night was because his son had come to this one. And his son only came because it had become more than a take-it-or-leave-it weekly activity. It had become an attractive *event* that he didn't want to miss.

If we tried to do what we were doing every week, then we couldn't have created the experience we had created. We couldn't have been as creative. We couldn't have spent as much money. We couldn't have spread the word as well as we did. We would've had fewer students in attendance because it would've generated less interest.

The experience was so positive because we had extra money to spend, drew more people to attend, and communicated the details in ways that made students remember.

Technically, there wasn't anything wrong with the events we had been doing every Sunday night. Parents were happy with it. A few students attended it. But I wasn't satisfied with it. I knew that by narrowing our focus we could do better. Andy Stanley explains, "Narrowing your focus means you choose what potentially works best over what is presently working."[53]

I believed that we could reach more students and have a better time together if we scaled back. Fortunately, I was right. We were able to reach more students by doing fewer things.

YOUR MOVE

Think through your programs. Are they accomplishing the purpose for which they were started in the first place? Are there any programs that you can eliminate? Are there any that you can scale back in order to accomplish more? Are there any that could be shifted from weekly to monthly?

Also, consider how many times you're asking students to show up at your church in a given week. Most of your students probably don't have their driver's license yet, so that means you're asking their parents to drive them. With the number of dual-income households on the rise, you might find that you're asking them to attend too much, too often.

Don't believe the idea that you have to do more things in order to reach more students. It's not true. Doing too much spreads your time, energy, and resources too thin to make everything as good as it needs to be. Instead, narrow your focus. Focus on those few things that make the biggest difference, and do those things to the best of your ability.

STRATEGY #15:

Accomplish more by doing less.

CHAPTER 16
WHY YOUR STUDENTS DON'T SING (AND WHAT YOU CAN DO ABOUT IT)

From time to time, I ask our volunteers to evaluate how things are going in our ministry. They rate different aspects of our large group and small group time on a scale of 1 through 5.

Across the board, the lowest rating has been for students singing during the worship time.

That naturally leads to the question: *Why aren't students singing?*

Then there's a follow-up question: *What can I do about it?*

I have a few thoughts that I'll share to answer those questions.

5 REASONS WHY YOUR STUDENTS DON'T SING

1. THEY'RE EMBARRASSED

Why is it that girls who are perfectly fine singing the latest

Katy Perry song at the top of their lungs at a slumber party, suddenly clam up at church when the band plays the latest song by Hillsong?

I think it's because everyone knows they're playing around at the slumber party. It doesn't matter that they sing off-key or out of tune. They're just singing and laughing.

But at church, they think they're supposed to be serious and reverent. They're expected to at least *try* to sing well. But how many of us can really carry a tune? Not many. Instead of trying to sound good and failing, they would rather not sing at all. They don't want to embarrass themselves.

It's one thing to be told you can't sing when you're not trying. It's another thing to be told you can't sing when you're really trying. Rather than risk their reputations, some students simply refrain from singing at all.

WHAT CAN YOU DO ABOUT IT?

Turn up the volume.

Maybe it's just me, but I will sing when I can't hear myself sing. For that to happen, the volume needs to be turned up. And when the band stops playing and the worship leader backs away from the mic and says, "Just your voices now," I don't feel inclined to belt out the next lyric. It's just the opposite, actually. I feel inclined to wait for the band to start playing and the worship leader to start singing again before I keep going.

One way to help students fight embarrassment is to turn up the volume. That way, they aren't worried that the person next to them is listening to them and judging how they sound.

WHAT ELSE CAN YOU DO ABOUT IT?

Teach a series about worship.

Talk to your students about what worship is and why we do it. Teach students about how the songs we sing shape the thoughts we think and the truths we believe. Worship is more than singing songs, but singing songs together has been a significant part of worship for thousands of years. Help students see their singing within that larger context by teaching why it matters.

2. THEY DON'T KNOW THE SONGS

Because new worship songs come out every month, I think our temptation is to phase out the older songs too quickly. Then we wonder why our students aren't singing. They aren't singing because they can't sing a song they don't know. Even if the words are on the screen for them, they need to hear the song a few times before they can sing it from the heart.

Here's what typically happens:

We introduce new songs to our students. It takes a few weeks, but they begin to learn them. They start to sing along. And then, just when they're beginning to really engage with God through those songs, we move on to other new songs.

We're moving too quickly. Those songs haven't had the chance to make a deep impression on our students yet. Slow down. Just because your musicians are getting tired of playing a song doesn't mean you should move it out of the rotation. In fact, when your musicians get tired of playing a song, your students have probably just started to engage with it.

WHAT CAN YOU DO ABOUT IT?

Play no more than fifteen different songs each semester.

Before the semester starts, pick fifteen songs that you think your students will connect with. You'll want to classify them according to theme and tempo, so you don't end up with too many slow songs or not enough reflective songs on the list. Ideally, you will have your teaching calendar filled out, and you can select songs with lyrics that highlight the themes you'll be talking about.

As an added benefit, when you create a song list for the semester, your musicians will play better because they will have more practice playing the songs together. Instead of having to learn new songs each week, they'll be able to get really good at playing the ones they already know.

When your students are singing songs they know, they won't have to focus on reading the words off the screen. When your musicians are playing songs they already know, they won't have to focus on reading the words off the music stand. That will free up both your students and your musicians to focus on the God they're singing about.

3. THE BAND IS BAD

I worked at a church that had a student praise band leading worship on Wednesday nights. The church wasn't big, so we didn't have a lot of students who were capable of playing instruments and singing very well. We used what we had, but what we had wasn't very good.

Should you blame students for not singing along when the music isn't good? I don't think so.

It's hard to sing along when the tempo is inconsistent, the

lyric slides have typos, and the kid playing guitar keeps doing his own thing.

WHAT CAN YOU DO ABOUT IT?

Schedule the band to play less.

There's no rule that says you have to include music every time you meet. In fact, if your band isn't very good, it can actually be beneficial to have them play less.

Maybe have them play one time per month instead of every week. That way, they'll have more time to practice the songs and get everything cleaned up before it's time to play.

If you feel like you absolutely must have music, then you can do something I've seen work very well with students: play worship songs through the speakers with lyrics on the screen (or use lyric videos). The key is to explain what you're doing and why it matters (just like a worship leader would do before the first song). Then, step aside, play the track, and let the students sing along.

WHAT ELSE CAN YOU DO ABOUT IT?

Ask experienced musicians to play alongside students.

You probably have access to some experienced musicians. Ask them to come to your band practice and help your students. Beyond that, ask them to come and play with them.

One time, I had to build a student band from scratch. It was either that or we wouldn't be able to do music at all. I heard about a husband and wife who worked at a church that was two hours away from mine. They helped train student praise bands. I drove up to meet them. We talked, and it turned out they knew a guy who lived in my town who could help us out.

I met with that guy and found out that he was willing to come and help our students. Not only that, but he didn't have anything else to do on Wednesday nights, so he even came out and played with them too!

People are willing to help. You just have to find them. Even if it takes driving two hours away to find someone who lives just down the road.

4. Leaders Aren't Singing

Ralph Waldo Emerson said, "The speed of the leader determines the pace of the pack." You and your leaders are setting the example for your students to follow.

If you aren't singing, how can you expect your students to sing?

If your leaders are huddled against the back wall talking, how can you expect your students to sing?

I felt sorry for the worship leader at one of the churches I worked at. He was on the stage, trying to lead the congregation as best he could. But he couldn't seem to get any traction. Hardly anyone was singing along. He was discouraged because he couldn't figure out what the problem was.

I knew what the problem was: the senior pastor would sit on the front pew, reviewing his sermon notes, while the rest of the congregation was supposed to be singing. If the leader wasn't interested in singing, neither was anyone else.

WHAT CAN YOU DO ABOUT IT?

Be an example for your students.

You don't need to call attention to yourself or make a public display of the fact that you're singing, but you do need to be visible. Students shouldn't just hear you talk about the importance of worshipping during the music; they should see you living it out and participating in it.

You should also explain to your leaders why their participation is so important. As leaders in your ministry, they aren't just there to perform their volunteer role. They're there to lead students by their example. When students see leaders clapping, singing, and participating, they will follow suit.

5. THE WORSHIP LEADER HASN'T ENGAGED THEM

I've seen it happen a hundred times. The person leading the songs takes on the role of music performer rather than worship leader. A music performer is basically the same as the lead singer of a cover band. That's essentially what's happening when someone performs a Chris Tomlin song without engaging people to join in the worship experience.

A worship leader knows it's his or her responsibility and privilege to help people encounter God in that moment. That's very different from just performing a song. The worship leader's goal is to move students from observation to participation.

Getting students to participate can be accomplished by something as simple as telling students that singing is an opportunity for them to express their hearts to God. It can be done at the start of the worship set by saying something like, "Take a second and think about what you're offering to God in these songs. You're offering your passion, devotion, and praise. You're offering all of who you are for all of who God is. That's a good trade."

WHAT CAN YOU DO ABOUT IT?

Use lyrics to set up the song.

Take a few seconds before a song to call attention to a lyric that has special importance. This is especially true for newer songs, but it's even helpful for songs your students already know. For example, in "Whom Shall I Fear (God of Angel Armies)" by Chris Tomlin, the worship leader could say:

"We're about to sing a song that declares the faithfulness of God. When things seem stacked against you, when they don't go your way, this is a declaration that God is with you and he is for you. He is faithful. His promises will not be broken. And because of that, there's no need to fear anything or anyone.

There's a line in this song that says, 'Whom shall I fear?' The answer is no one and nothing. Nothing can come between you and the powerful love of God for you. So, no matter what comes your way, you can rest assured that God is with you and God is for you. Do you believe that? Alright! Let's sing together."

When they get to that part of the song, students will recognize those lyrics and be gripped by them in a new way because the worship leader has taken the time to explain what they mean. The song will take on greater significance and students will be engaged as a result.

WHAT ELSE CAN YOU DO ABOUT IT?

Tell the worship leader to engage the students.

This sounds direct, but I'm shocked by how many worship leaders forget that their job isn't to perform the song flawlessly; their job is to lead the students in worship. If we wanted a flawless performance of the song, all we need to do is play the mp3.

The reason a worship leader is better than an mp3 is that the worship leader is there in the room. He or she can sense when students are engaged and when they aren't. A simple gesture made by the worship leader telling the students to clap their hands will get a few more students engaged than before. Saying something like, "Let me hear you sing it out" as the song enters the chorus will also help. And when a song is over, a nice compliment like "You guys sound great today," will go a long way toward getting them to open up and sing more.

YOUR MOVE

Helping your students sing praises to God is a significant part of youth ministry. Song lyrics provide words that are not readily available to students. When students don't know how to express the desire of their souls or the hurt in their hearts, song lyrics come to their rescue. When we fail to create an environment that is conducive to singing, we do a disservice to our students.

To summarize, my suggestions for helping students sing are:

- Turn up the volume.
- Teach a series about worship.
- Play no more than fifteen different songs each semester.

- Find experienced musicians.
- Be an example.
- Use lyrics to set up the song.
- Tell the worship leader to engage the students.

The suggestions I've given you here aren't the only ways to encourage students to sing, but they are a good start.

STRATEGY #16:

Help students express their worship through singing.

CHAPTER 17
MAKE THEM SAY "WOW!"

At Christmas time, my wife and I take our kids to Callaway Gardens to see the Fantasy in Lights. According to *National Geographic Traveler*, it's one of the top ten places to see holiday lights in the world. For the past twenty years, Callaway Gardens has set up eight million lights to dazzle their patrons and fill them with Christmas cheer.

As we're passing the giant Toy Soldiers or moving slowly through the Snowflake Valley, one word is on repeat in my kids' mouths: "Wow!" Then, on the way home, they're already asking if we can go back again next year.

When it comes to your ministry programs, you want your students to say, "Wow! I'm glad I came." You want them asking their parents to bring them back again. You want them to talk about it the next day at school. You want the students who weren't there to say, "Wow! I wish I would've been there." But that doesn't happen by accident. You have to plan for it.

HOW TO MAKE STUDENTS SAY "WOW!"

1. PLAN AHEAD

Don't wait until Monday morning to think about Wednesday night. The easiest way to get ahead is to create a preaching calendar for the next three months. Then create a folder on your computer or in Evernote with those dates and topics. Begin collecting ideas for hosting bits, games, videos, and teaching illustrations that connect with either a teaching theme or seasonal theme that is coming up.

For example, did you know that July 23rd is National Hot Dog Day? When I found that out, I made a note in my program files. Then, as that day was approaching, I came across a news story about the Hot Dog Eating Championship. The most recent winner was a guy named Matt Stonie. It turns out that he also makes YouTube videos of himself eating various foods. On one of those videos, he's eating as many Twinkies as he can in 60 seconds.

That gave me a great idea: I'd start off talking about National Hot Dog Day. I'd tell everyone about the new champion, Matt Stonie. Then I'd show his Twinkie video. We'd follow that with a Twinkie eating contest for students!

Do you see how that works? Did anyone eat more Twinkies in one minute than Matt Stonie? Nope. But they had a great time trying!

Plan ahead and you'll find tons of great ideas along the way.

2. MAKE IT FUN

I believe that helping students have fun is one of your

highest priorities as a youth pastor. But having fun isn't limited to games. Think of ways to help students laugh.

How can you take them by surprise?

What can you do to shake things up?

One summer, we set up a bubble blower outside the door where students came into the building. They loved it! They chased those bubbles all over the place just to try to pop them.

What if you switch your service around? You could start with a message and end with singing.

You could clear out the chairs and have your students sit on the floor. You could set up the chairs in a different way. You could do a planned interruption with a crazy character who tells everyone about upcoming events. You could show a hilarious Tripp and Tyler video.

Fun helps build trust, relationships, and engagement. You definitely want those things happening in your program. Those are the kinds of things that make students say "Wow!"

3. Mind the Gaps

As you put together your plan, be aware of the gaps. Gaps are those dead spots that happen during transitions. It's not cool when the countdown timer ends, and no one is on the stage. You don't want awkward silence when the game is over, and the band is still making its way onto the stage. There's a reason it's called *awkward*.

Use a mixer question to give the band time to get on stage. Use a transition video to allow time for the band to exit the stage while the speaker gets into position. If you're using a video clip during your message, make sure the person running the computer knows when it's supposed to play. If you're using a prop, make sure you don't have to leave the stage to get it at the crucial moment.

Also, think about what happens when the program is over. I've seen services end while the sound guy fumbles through Spotify to find the right playlist. Again, awkward silence. Those gaps have the potential to kill the momentum you've created, so take the time to think through those moments of transition when you're planning your programs.

Your Move

These three principles involve preparation. Students can tell when you've prepared for them and when you haven't. If you get up and just wing it, they'll know. And they won't be impressed. They probably won't want to come back.

When you prepare, it shows you care. When students can see that you've prepared for them, they're more likely to believe that you care about them. And when they believe that you care about them, they're more likely to listen to what you tell them.

That's why this is so important. Planning programs that make students say "Wow!" isn't an optional add-on to an otherwise good youth ministry. It's an essential part of what makes a youth ministry good in the first place.

STRATEGY #17:

Make students say "Wow!"

CHAPTER 18
4 EVALUATION QUESTIONS TO ASK AFTER YOUR NEXT SERVICE

Sunday comes every seven days. Wednesday night happens every week. You put a ton of effort into making your programs the best that they can be. You planned and prepared all week. And then the day comes. Your group meets. You execute your plan and do as well as you can. And then it's over; students go home.

You did your best. The results are what they are. You can't change them; you can only learn from them.

What should you do next? It's time to evaluate.

LEARNING FROM THE NFL

Where do you think NFL players are on Monday morning? They're in the film room, watching the video from Sunday's game. Marc Lillibridge, a former NFL player, explains, "Every player starts the week after a game by breaking down the previous game as a unit or in positional meetings...The previous week's game is dissected and graded."[54]

In that meeting, teams don't just focus on the negatives. Those things are discussed, but they also spend time highlighting the positives too. Lillibridge remembers, "One of my favorite parts of watching game film as a team was good plays by individual players...While ESPN may focus on the highlights, NFL players focus on the jobs they are asked to do on any one play."[55]

The purpose of evaluation isn't to make anyone feel bad; it's to help everyone get better. Sometimes you recognize things that need to be celebrated. Other times, you see things that need to be corrected. Either way, the point of evaluating things is to make them better.

It's easy to get caught in the cycle of doing the same things in the same ways. Anyone can get stuck in a rut. It takes intentional, directed effort to stay focused on making continuous improvements that make your services as good as they can be.

These four questions can help you do that. Ask them after your next service.

4 EVALUATION QUESTIONS

1. WHAT WENT RIGHT?

You need to celebrate all of the things that worked well. The game that worked perfectly is something to celebrate. It could be the bottom line of your message that landed with just the right sense of importance and empowerment. The volunteers who hung out with students after the service was over should be celebrated.

You can't repeat the things that went right if you don't take a few minutes to think about why they worked so well.

2. What Went Wrong?

You need to fix the things that didn't work. These are usually obvious to everyone who was in the room. Maybe the band wasn't in place when the countdown timer hit zero. If the same student has been picked to play in the upfront game for the last three weeks, you need to figure out how to keep that from happening again. Maybe the person in charge of your slides didn't follow your talk very well, and you had to keep saying, "Go to the next one."

When you identify what went wrong, you can make it better for next time.

3. What Was Missing?

You need to figure out what wasn't happening that should've been happening. These things usually aren't obvious. Unlike the things that went wrong, things that are missing simply weren't there to notice in the first place. But they should've been.

Maybe students were looking bored before the program started. Is there anything you can do to create pre-service engagement? You could set up a café and sell some snacks and drinks to help them feel more comfortable. Or you could have trivia questions scrolling on the screens in the room.

Maybe you were only supposed to speak for twenty minutes, but you got carried away and went on for thirty-two minutes. You need to add a clock to the back wall. Or you could have someone in the back of the room wave their hand when you have five minutes left.

When you add things that were missing, you fill in the gaps and create a more enjoyable, attractive experience for your students.

4. What Was Confusing?

The confusing parts usually happen during the check-in, the announcements, the game, the message, or the dismissal. During check-in, do you want everyone to check in or just new students? If you give them a form to fill out, what should they do with it when they're done? Where should they go when they're done checking in? Is there any place that is off-limits for them?

During the announcements, make sure you communicate clearly. If you have a group that is getting together at Dave's house on Friday night, give them Dave's address. Better still, put it on a slide and tell your students to take a picture of it with their phones. That way, parents won't have to call you on Friday night to ask where Dave lives.

Also, get creative with your announcements. Students miss a lot of announcements because they're talking about other stuff with their friends. Get their attention. Say something like, "Ok, if you're a middle school girl raise your left hand in the air. If your left hand is in the air right now, that means you're a middle school girl, and this announcement is for you."

Games can be confusing too. This is the time to sort that out. During the game, did students know exactly how to play? Was anything unclear?

During the message, did students understand your main point? Was it memorable? Did you offer a clear next step or call to action for students?

During the dismissal, did you tell students what to do next? Do you want them to stay in the room until their parents arrive to pick them up? Do you want them to wait outside? Do you want everyone to meet up afterward at a local restaurant? Those details are often confusing because they're left unsaid.

Think about what was confusing, and try to bring clarity to those things next time.

Your Move

After your next service, ask these four questions. They will help you get better every single week. All you have to do is ask them, answer them honestly, and work to make things better.

Again, those questions are:

- What went right?
- What went wrong?
- What was missing?
- What was confusing?

Once every month, you might even consider sending these questions to your volunteers on the day after your service. I have included a form in the Bonus Material that you can give them for this. Your volunteers can offer some valuable feedback that can help you make important improvements that you might not have otherwise considered.

STRATEGY #18:

Take time to think about what happened and why.

CHAPTER 19

A FOOL-PROOF SYSTEM TO FOLLOW UP WITH NEW STUDENTS

You work really hard to attract new students to your ministry. You challenge your students to invite their friends. You host big events. You try to make your programs better.

And then it happens. New students show up! That's exciting.

But your job isn't done at that point. You want them to come back next week too. The way you make that happen is with a follow-up system. How you follow up determines whether or not you'll see those new students again.

If you don't have a follow-up process, you're not doing yourself any favors. Students will come to your ministry, and you'll never see them again. Even if they have a good time, most of them still won't come back.

If you want new students to consistently come back to your church, you need a follow-up system. The key word is "consistently."

Every youth pastor can offer an example of an outlier: the student who came back on their own without follow-up. But that's the exception, not the rule. If you want a high percentage of students consistently coming back to your ministry, then you need a follow-up system. Let me put it this way: I've never seen a high percentage of students consistently coming back to a ministry without a follow-up system.

If you want to see student after student returning to your ministry week after week, then you need to have a system.

Do you have a system to do that?

Here's the follow-up system that I've used to triple the attendance in three different ministries.

THE FOOL-PROOF FOLLOW-UP SYSTEM

1. HAVE A CHECK-IN TABLE

The key to following up starts at check-in. You want to have an open, inviting, uncluttered table where new students check-in.

There are two types of new students who visit your ministry:

a. Students who come with their family.

b. Students who come with their friend.

Our students meet upstairs in our building. To create more awareness, we have adult volunteers in place downstairs to greet new families and let them know that students meet upstairs. If they come with their friend, they'll already know where to go.

We also have adult volunteers at the check-in table

upstairs. It's the first thing that students see when they walk up the stairs. On the check-in table, there are three things:

a. About You Form

b. About Our Ministry Card

c. My business card

We ask every new student to fill out the About You Form. The adult volunteer needs to watch to make sure the student's handwriting is legible. If it's not, then the volunteer can simply write the information on the card for them. That gets the ball rolling for the Follow-Up System to begin. Without that information, you won't be able to follow up.

By the way, I have included examples for everything I mention in this chapter in the Bonus Material for this book.

2. Make a Connection

Our model is unique. We meet for large group and small group on Sunday mornings, both during the same service. Large group lasts for 35 minutes; small group lasts for the remaining 30 minutes. Because of that, it's important to connect new students with their small group leader right away.

A member of our volunteer Host Team will take the new student from the table into the room and introduce them to their small group leader.

If your model is different, that's fine. Your Host Team volunteer would escort the new student into the student area and introduce them to some students from their school or in their grade.

Because the Host Team volunteer will leave the check-in table in order to connect the new student, it is important that you always have at least two volunteers scheduled to work at your check-in table. That way, the table isn't empty when another new student shows up.

3. Send a Card

On Monday morning, I take a few minutes to write a card to every student who attended for the first time. The card is a basic, white card with our logo on the front. It's blank on the inside. Here's an example of what I write:

"Hey Maria, I'm so glad that you came and hung out with us on Sunday! I hope you had a good time and met some really nice people. Hopefully we'll see you again soon!"

I also include two things:

a. *Social Media Card.* This is a small, square card that lists where the student can find us on social media.

b. *Free T-Shirt Card.* This card promises the student a free t-shirt when they come back with the card. Some youth ministries will give a t-shirt or some other gift to every student who attends for the first time. I don't do that because I don't want to give a shirt to someone's cousin who is visiting from three hours away. My budget isn't *that* big! Plus, I expect students to have a really good experience when they come for the first time. Offering them a free t-shirt when they come back is a great way to entice them to come back again. I can't use that as leverage if I give them the goodies on their first visit.

4. Email Parents

On the About You Form, I include a space for their parent's

email address. Some students don't know their parent's email address, but some do. When I get a parent's email address, I send them an email like this:

> "Hi Mrs. Johnson, I just wanted to let you know that it was a pleasure having Brandon attend our church last Sunday. He seems like a great young man. If I can ever help your family in any way, please let me know. Would it be alright if I add you to our email list to keep you informed about what we're teaching and doing in our student ministry? Just let me know. We do a lot of fun things and I don't want Brandon to miss out. Hopefully we'll see you again soon!"

I use MailChimp for our email list because it's free, simple to set up, and easy to use. It's important to send regular emails to parents (at least once every month) because it's a great way to keep them in the loop about what you've been teaching or events that are just around the corner.

5. SEND A BIRTHDAY CARD

This is a simple gesture that makes a big impression on students. A student's birthday is a natural time for you to connect with them. I send a birthday card to *every* student who has ever visited our church. It's not overbearing, and it doesn't feel like you have ulterior motives. You're just saying, "Happy Birthday!"

They tell you their birthday on the About You Form. It's not hard for you to jot it down in your calendar with an alert to remind you two days before. That will give you enough time to write the card and put it in the mail.

I do not recommend sending out all of the month's

birthday cards at the beginning of the month. It seems impersonal and too automated. Instead, you want the birthday card to show up in the student's mailbox on their birthday. Or, at least, as close as you can get it to their birthday. That level of attention to detail demonstrates a personal touch that shows the student you really care.

I also include a $5 gift card to the Great American Cookie Company in each birthday card I send. I recommend you do something similar. This simple addition is what will set your gesture apart from every other person who randomly tells them happy birthday because they saw everyone else doing it on social media.

Depending on your budget, you might not be able to do that, but I think it's a very small investment that has the potential to go a very long way toward a student's positive perception of your ministry.

The cards I use are the same ones that I send to first-time attenders. I just write a birthday message instead. Here's an example of what I write:

"Hey Jake, Happy Birthday!! We hope your birthday is as awesome as you are!" I sign it from *"Your Friends at [x Ministry]."*

Again, I have used this system in three different churches. The response is always amazing. I've had students show up a few weeks after they visited for the first time and tell me that my note meant a lot to them because they had never received anything like that before. I've also had students who visited six months earlier show back up because they received a birthday card from me. They hadn't thought about church in a while, but they wanted to come back and check it out.

YOUR MOVE

My guess is that you have several new students coming to your church every month. I developed this system for following up with new students through several years of trial and error. I was tired of inconsistent follow-up. I wanted a system that I could put in place and get results. That's what this Follow-Up System did for me.

If you don't have a system to follow up with new students, or if your system isn't working very well, I would encourage you to adopt this one. You'll see students coming back to your ministry like never before!

The system works, so work the system.

STRATEGY #19:

Follow up with every new student
who attends your ministry.

CHAPTER 20

IS YOUR YOUTH ROOM DRIVING STUDENTS AWAY?

I received an invitation to speak at a high school. It was a student-led Christian group that gathers before school starts on Wednesday morning. You know the kind. You've probably spoken to groups like that. It's a standard part of being a youth pastor.

When I walked into the room (which wasn't easy to find), I was greeted by a nice student. He was a junior at the school. He was tall with brown hair, wearing preppy clothes. He told me how the morning would go:

"We'll start with announcements. Then a prayer. Elijah will play his keyboard and lead us in three songs. Hopefully, he'll get here on time. Then you'll be up. After you speak, I'll come back up to dismiss everyone."

It sounded fine to me. It probably sounds okay to you too, right? With the exception of a game, it probably sounds about like your typical Wednesday night program.

WHAT I NOTICED

As I waited for everything to get started, I noticed some things:

There were random scribbles on the big whiteboard in the front of the room. Chairs were scattered in a disorderly way. On the opposite side of the random scribbles, someone had written the social media information for the group on the board. Either that person had really bad handwriting, or they were in a big hurry because I could barely read it.

A girl was working quickly at the computer. I asked her what she was up to. She was copying song lyrics from websites and pasting them into a Word document that would be displayed through the projector for the singing part of the morning. There would turn out to be several typos in those lyrics.

I noticed that it was quiet. Too quiet. And awfully bright. There wasn't any music playing, and every one of the fluorescent lights that hung on the low-hanging ceiling tiles was turned on.

I wondered where all of the students were. I'd been told there would be around fifty of them here. I saw closer to fifteen. Not only was there a shortage of students, but there was also a noticeable lack of food. There weren't any snacks. Not a single breakfast pastry could be found. Nor were there any bottles of water or juice available.

I found the leader of the group again. "I thought you said there would be around fifty students here. Where is everyone?"

"Well, we had that many coming a while ago, but a lot of them stopped coming," he said.

"Are you seeing any new people show up?" I asked.

"Not in the last few months," he said. "I'm not sure why."

As I looked around, I wasn't surprised. I knew exactly why. And you can probably guess the reasons.

WHAT'S THE POINT?

I share this experience because I think that if you switch the setting from a school on a Wednesday morning to your church on a Wednesday night, the situation might sound eerily familiar.

Here's the point: Your place matters.

In fact, the first step to building a better youth ministry – in my opinion – is to create a place that is appealing to students. Without an appealing place, students simply won't show up.

That shouldn't be controversial, but every now and then I hear youth pastors say things like, "If kids really love God, then they'll show up." Or, "Christians in Africa worship in churches that have mud floors and no air conditioning. Our students should be grateful to have what they have."

I agree, students *should* be grateful. Our culture and country allow us to have many luxuries. But I must point out that we're not in Africa, so it doesn't help to compare their situation with ours. In America, we're trying to reach American students.

YOUR YOUTH ROOM MATTERS

One summer, the air conditioning in our student building stopped working. I asked the church facilities manager to get it fixed. Weeks went by, but it didn't get fixed. One night during the program, a student came up to me and complained, "It's 87 degrees in here!"

Was it petty for that student to complain about that? I don't think so.

Your youth room matters. Can we all agree on that? That's not wrong to say. Neither is it new. Even Charles Spurgeon, the great British preacher of the 19th century, said, "Frequently it is very difficult for congregations to attend because of the place and the atmosphere."[56]

If you want students to enjoy coming to your church, look forward to being there, and feel good about inviting their friends, then you have to pay attention to your place. It was true for Spurgeon in the 19th century, and it's true for you today in the 21st century.

CASE STUDY: PROBLEMS & SOLUTIONS

So, let's go back to that high school club and use it as a case study. What is going wrong and how can it be fixed?

PROBLEM #1:

The room wasn't easy to find.

SOLUTION #1:

Create a team of greeters. Give them matching shirts with the group name or logo on it. Station them at key areas where people could potentially take a wrong turn. Plus, you could get a sign made. Nothing fancy, just a simple A-frame sign would be fine. Put it in front of the room so it can be seen down a long hallway of classrooms that all look the same.

PROBLEM #2:

No snacks or drinks

SOLUTION #2:

Get a parent to be in charge of finding and scheduling other parents who would be willing to provide refreshments on a weekly rotation. Or, you could reach out to a local bakery or bagel shop and ask them for their day-old items that would otherwise by thrown away. You could even bring a bunch of Chick-fil-A biscuits on the first week of each month and ask students to pay for them. They'll gladly do it.

PROBLEM #3:

Random scribbles on the whiteboard.

SOLUTION #3:

Take some pride in your place and pay attention to details. Find an eraser and remove things that aren't relevant to what you're doing that day. This is also true for outdated material. Whenever I visit churches, I usually find promotional flyers for events that happened over a month ago. Clean up and get rid of that stuff.

PROBLEM #4:

Illegible social media information

SOLUTION #4:

Either print the information on small, attractive cards to hand out each week, or find an artistic student with good handwriting to make it look fresh and clean on the board. You've probably seen this done in coffee shop windows. They don't just scribble their specials on the window. They find someone who knows how to draw to make it look nice and appealing.

PROBLEM #5:

Disorderly chairs

SOLUTION #5:

Decide if you want rows or a circle, and set up the chairs that way. Make sure that unused chairs are out of the way. On that note, it's better to set up too few chairs than too many. If you set up too many chairs, then it looks like you were expecting more people to show up and raises the question of why they didn't. If you set up too few chairs, then it looks like something good is happening because more people showed up than you were expecting.

PROBLEM #6:

The room is too quiet.

SOLUTION #6:

Play some music as people are coming in and hanging out before things get started. If you're in a room without a sound system, then buy a portable Bluetooth speaker and connect your phone to it. Upbeat music is best. Your program isn't a funeral, so play some songs that get people feeling good.

When it comes to music, one of the questions youth pastors often ask me is whether or not they should play secular music. My answer is simple: it depends on the program. If the program is designed to reach non-Christian students (typically Wednesday night in most churches), then I don't see any problem with playing songs they hear on the radio. Just don't pick ones with explicit lyrics or questionable content. There are plenty of songs that have a good beat and a positive message that aren't distinctly Christian. Playing those songs says to new students that you know what's going on in their world. You aren't irrelevant, and neither is your message.

On the other hand, if the program is designed to educate Christian students (typically Sunday morning in most churches), then I would play contemporary, upbeat Christian music. Most students know what's popular on the radio, but they don't know about good Christian music. I want to give them a taste of what else is out there. Playing those songs says to Christian students that our message isn't irrelevant, and neither is our music.

PROBLEM #7:

The room is too bright.

SOLUTION #7:

Turn on only half of the overhead lights. Or, better still, go to the store and get a few floor lamps. Lighting sets the mood. You want the room to feel inviting and warm. Less like a hospital, more like a coffee shop.

The issue of the typos in the song lyrics is also a problem, but I'll let it pass because it isn't relevant to this topic. Suffice it to say, make sure your song lyrics are easy to read and typo-free.

YOUR MOVE

As you can tell, none of these solutions is very hard to do. They can be implemented very easily, without spending a lot of money. It just takes a willingness to pay attention and make adjustments.

As you read through the list of problems and solutions, did anything stick out to you that might be happening in your youth room?

Keep your eyes open. Pay attention to what you see. Imagine things through the eyes of a guest who isn't familiar with your place.

What if you were walking into that room for the very first time?

- Would you feel excited?
- Would you feel awkward?
- Would you feel comfortable?
- Would you want to come back?

As I participated in the program that morning at the high school club, I felt like things ran smoothly. I don't think the reason why students stopped showing up is because the program is bad. I think it has more to do with the environment they've created. Their biggest problem is their place. But, with some attention to detail, that can be fixed.

STRATEGY #20:

Create a space where students want to meet.

CHAPTER 21
LITTLE THINGS THAT MAKE A BIG DIFFERENCE WITH STUDENTS

I know of a church that spent over $1 million on a new student building, and it was absolutely amazing. It had everything you could dream of: cool furniture, a big café area, expensive video, sound, and lighting equipment. They hadn't skimped on anything. But the youth pastor called me because they had a problem.

He explained the situation: "We built this incredible building to reach more students. We wanted to send a message to our community that we value the next generation. But ever since we opened it, our student attendance has gone down, not up."

He was totally confused about how that could be happening. I agreed to go and check things out. After visiting the church and having several conversations with staff, students, and volunteers, the problem was clear: they were relying on the building to do the work of a person.

BUILDINGS AREN'T PEOPLE

Big problems happen when youth pastors expect buildings to reach students, and they stop doing their part to care for the students who attend. Students want three things more than anything else in the world: to be seen, heard, and understood. Buildings can't do any of those things.

Tim Cool is a facility designer who has helped more than 350 churches throughout the United States. He cautions church leaders about the limits of what a new building can do by explaining, "Facilities are merely tools to assist a church or ministry to fulfill its vision."[57] In other words, don't expect a building to do your work for you. It's just a tool.

If you don't help every student feel special and cared about, then every time you see new students coming into your ministry, you'll also see other students leaving it.

They won't announce that they're leaving. They'll just slowly drift away. They'll stop showing up. They'll wonder if anyone notices. After a while, they'll just stop coming altogether.

So, in your haste to grow your group, it's helpful to slow down and remember that ministry is all about people. It won't do you any good to have a clear vision, a cool band, and a state-of-the-art sound system if you forget the reason you're in ministry in the first place: to serve people and point them to Jesus.

Sure, a new building will attract a few new students in the first month that it's open. But after that, you'll have the same students you had before if you don't make it unmistakably clear to your students that you care about them.

How can you do that?

21 WAYS TO SHOW STUDENTS YOU CARE

1. REMEMBER THEIR NAMES

Saying, "Hey man" isn't good enough. Make an effort to learn students' names and use their names when you're talking to them.

2. PRAY FOR THEM BY NAME

Don't just pray generalized prayers for your group. Pick a few students and pray for them by name each day.

3. FOLLOW UP AFTER PRAYER REQUESTS

When a student asks you to pray for something, ask them about it later. Don't just leave it in the past. Bring it up the next time you see them, and they'll know you really care.

4. MEET THEM FOR BREAKFAST

Set your alarm clock, get up early, and meet a student for breakfast. You'll be amazed how much they'll share about what's really happening in their lives when it's just the two of you eating a biscuit together.

5. TAKE LUNCH TO THEM

Different school districts have different rules about this kind of thing, but if you're allowed to take lunch to students at school, do it. Ask them what they want to eat, show up with it, and sit down at the table. They'll love it! If you can't take lunch to their school, then coordinate with their parents and surprise them with a pizza at their house on a Saturday!

6. Ask for Their Sports Schedules

Students have a life outside of church. You want them to care about what you're doing at church, so show an interest in what they're doing outside of church.

7. Go See Their Games and Events

It's not enough just to ask for a schedule. Put some dates on your calendar and make it a point to get there and cheer them on. If you don't spend any time with your students outside of your church, don't be surprised when they decide not to spend any time at your church.

8. Brag On Them to Their Parents

Parents never get tired of hearing how well their kids are doing. Tell them about the ways you've seen their student grow over the past year. Talk about the character qualities they're developing. Give them examples of what you've seen.

9. Brag On Their Parents to Them

Adolescence brings changes to the parent-child relationship. Students create distance from their parents and try to establish themselves as individuals. That's fine; it's normal. Remind your students that their parents love them and want the best for them.

10. Build Them Up in Front of Their Friends

Students are extremely self-conscious. They will do almost anything to try to fit in. When you see them talking with their friends, don't do anything that might humiliate or embarrass them. Instead, go out of your way to compliment them and help them feel like a big deal.

11. Send Them a Birthday Card

There are only a few days in a student's life when he is the center of attention. His birthday is usually one of those days. Don't miss out on the chance to make students feel special on their birthday.

12. Ask Them to Babysit Your Kids

A student knows that you trust her when you ask her to babysit for your kids. You are giving her a sense of responsibility, plus a little money. Not only that, but you are inviting that student into your house to see how you really live. That gives you added credibility.

13. Send Them a Picture from an Event

When your group goes somewhere or does something, I'm sure you take pictures. If you don't, you should. You can post them on your social media accounts. But you'll make a bigger difference with a student if you choose a good picture of them, get it printed, and mail it to them in a card.

14. Listen When They Talk

If you want students to open up to you, then you have to give them your attention when they're talking to you. Don't let yourself get distracted. Don't check your phone. Don't check your watch. Don't interrupt. Just listen.

15. Notice When They're Not There

When a student doesn't show up, give them a call or send them a text just to check in with them. Let them know you missed them, and they're more likely to be there next time.

16. Be Real

Students can spot a fake from a mile away. Perfection isn't a high priority for today's teenagers, but authenticity is. They want straight talk and real answers to issues that are happening around them and to them. They value integrity and sincerity. They don't get that in most places or from most people. If they get it from you and your ministry, they'll keep coming back for more.

17. Encourage Them to Serve in the Church

Students who serve are students who stay. At the Orange Conference in 2015, Reggie Joiner said, "Students might outgrow your programs, but they'll never outgrow a personal ministry." When students serve, they feel a sense of responsibility and ownership that makes it harder to walk away.

18. Give Them Responsibilities in Your Ministry

Because you're the youth pastor, the temptation is to plan everything and do everything yourself. Don't give into that temptation. Let them help you plan. Let them run slides. Let them play in the band. Let them help with a game. Let them do announcements. Let them share a testimony. Let them teach part of your message. Responsibility creates buy-in. When students have responsibilities in your ministry, they'll have more buy-in to your ministry.

19. Challenge Them to Be Leaders

Many students get bored with their faith. They don't sense a challenge. They feel like they've arrived. Challenge those students to step up, step out, and lead the way for others.

20. Visit Them at Their Part-Time Jobs

As students get older, they venture out and get part-time jobs. You will absolutely make their day when you show up and see them in action. They will beam with pride when you walk through the door.

21. Give Them a Vision for Their Lives

Most students live in the moment. They have a small vision for what is possible in their lives. That's why they give into temptation so easily. They don't think very much is at stake. When you talk with a student, take a minute to cast a big vision for what you think they're capable of doing. Expand their thinking. Give them big goals. Raise their level of expectation.

KIND GESTURES AT THE RIGHT TIME

As I think about my life and faith so far, the big events and expensive buildings weren't the things that kept me close to Christ. The thing that helped me most has been the kind gestures that came from people at just the right time.

When I was a new Christian, I was caught between my old friends' expectations and trying to find new friends who supported my new identity. Some of the guys from church invited me on a road trip to see a concert with them. Those guys became my good friends and helped me get through that tricky time.

In college, a deacon from my church sent me a text message every Friday morning that said, "I'm praying for you. Let me know if I can do anything for you." Those prayers sustained me in that time.

In ministry, a parent will send an email that says, "Thank you for making a difference in my son's life." Those emails remind me that I'm doing important work.

Those are the kind gestures that came from people at just the right time for me. Those are the things that have kept me close to Christ through the years.

Your Move

As you're working on all the important tasks of ministry, don't give in to the temptation to rely on your talent and technology. If you do that, you'll be done when the church down the road gets better talent and newer technology than you have. You have to think beyond the stage and bigger than the building.

Be intentional about doing the things that build relationships and strengthen community among your students.

It's like Doug Fields says: "Youth ministry is about adults loving students, building relationships with them, and pointing them to Jesus."[58]

You never know when one of the students in your ministry will think back on their faith and remember a kind gesture that you made for them at just the right time.

STRATEGY #21:

Show students how much you care.

CHAPTER 22
WHY SERMONS MATTER SO MUCH

In their pursuit of fun games and planning future events, youth pastors don't always give their sermons the attention they deserve.

That's a mistake.

Your weekly sermon is one of the most important things that happens in your ministry. It would be better for you to have an engaging sermon and a boring game than a boring sermon and an engaging game.

Why is that?

Each week, when you get up to speak, you have an opportunity to set the tone and shape the culture of your ministry. The words you say – the verses you choose and the illustrations you use – can determine the quality of the choices your students make.

I don't want to minimize the other aspects of your ministry. I believe you should strive for excellence in everything your ministry does. But in talking with other youth pastors, I've begun to sense a trend: their sermons have taken a backseat to other stuff.

I also don't want to add pressure to your preaching. I don't believe that most of your students will remember what you said from one week to the next. But I do believe they will remember that you said it, and they believed it.

The point of your preaching is not to convince students to be faithful for the rest of their lives; the point is to convince them to be faithful for the rest of the week. Then, when you come back together next week, you must convince them again.

As the weeks build up and students grow up, that steady stream of sermons will have prepared those students for a lifetime of faithfulness. But it happens week after week, sermon after sermon.

One week of good preaching at summer camp can't undo fifty-one weeks of bad preaching in your youth ministry.

Do You Remember RadioShack?

The company was founded in 1921. It sold radio parts and random supplies, mostly through catalogs. It struggled for the first forty years before it was bought by Charles Tandy, the owner of a leather company who wanted to diversify his portfolio.

Tandy inherited a chain of nine existing RadioShack stores that were underperforming. He got to work, quickly identifying the 20% of the products that produced 80% of the sales revenue. He slashed the number of products from 40,000 from 2,500 and replaced the large retail stores with several smaller locations.

The changes worked.

New technologies were making their way into American homes, and people enjoyed tinkering with all the new possibilities. RadioShack focused its business on connecting with those do-it-yourself types. In its heyday, they had 7,000 stores across the country. According to one business writer, "RadioShack entered the 1980s poised to be the center of the computer revolution."[59]

There was just one problem: They lost their focus.

Charles Tandy died in 1978, and RadioShack left their core business in his absence. They chased after the next big thing but ended up with nothing. They tried computers but were beat out by IBM and Apple. They tried phones but lost to Motorola and AT&T. They tried boomboxes but were bested by Sony and JVC. More recently, they were undercut by Amazon and outperformed by Best Buy in everything they did.

In the final analysis, "RadioShack tried many paths. But going in all directions without a full commitment is not enough, particularly when the core brand is not sustained. RadioShack has branded itself well but it led itself too far from its strengths."[60] They filed for bankruptcy in 2015.

HOW ABOUT YOU?

Have you been giving your sermons the attention they deserve? RadioShack fell when they failed to focus on their core brand. I believe that the sermon is part of your core brand. Without a powerful sermon, you are simply gathering students for a fun time.

I know that's not why you're in ministry. You have been called by God to proclaim the message of the gospel. I'm a big fan of having fun in youth ministry, but all of the fun you work to create is a means to the end of proclaiming the message.

In a sermon, you use words to describe the God who creates, sustains, and redeems the world. With your words, you expose the lies and uncover the truth. Your words also empower students to join together for a cause that is bigger than themselves. That's what you're doing with every sermon you preach.

If you forget that, then people will eventually say the same things about your ministry that they're saying about RadioShack now: it had so much potential, but nothing ever came of it.

3 REASONS WHY SERMONS ARE SO IMPORTANT

1. IN YOUR SERMONS, YOU DESCRIBE GOD.

For a presentation to be a sermon, it must call attention to God. God is the creator, sustainer, and redeemer of the world. Life has value and purpose because it was God's idea.

This is the God who spoke, and creation was formed. This is the God who grieves over sin and loss. This is the God who revealed himself fully and finally in the person and work of Jesus Christ. This is the God who is coming to make all things new.

When you speak to students, tell them about the God who created, sustains, and redeems the world.

2. IN YOUR SERMONS, YOU EXPOSE THE LIES (AND UNCOVER THE TRUTH).

False narratives pervade the hallways of schools and brain-waves of students. Classmates and commercials combine to tell them that they aren't pretty enough, cool enough, smart enough, or strong enough to matter. Students are battered with advertising messages that say they don't have what it takes to make a difference. However, those advertisers are quick to point out that if students would use their products, then things could be different.

In your sermons, you have an opportunity to undo those lies. Expose them. Call them out. Name them and shame them. Replace those lies by offering a counter-narrative that uncovers the truth. According to C. S. Lewis, that counter-narrative is as follows:

"God made us: invented us as a man invents an engine... Now God designed the human machine to run on Himself. He Himself is the fuel our spirits were designed to burn, or the food our spirits were designed to feed on. There is no other."[61]

The search for purpose and belonging must begin with God, or it is doomed to fail. When you speak to students, help them see the lies and believe the truth.

3. IN YOUR SERMONS, YOU EMPOWER STUDENTS.

Your students want to be included in something that is bigger than themselves. When I speak to students, I want them to feel both uplifted and energized, not just as separate individuals but as a united group. I want them to understand that they are not on their own; they're together in the fight of faith. Part of that fight is to enlist them in work that matters.

Martin Luther described sin as "Man curved in on himself." That is a picture of the shrunken, solitary life. He could've simply referenced the story of Narcissus, the character from Greek mythology who was entranced by his own reflection. According to Eugene Peterson, "Narcissus got smaller and smaller until there was no Narcissus left: he had starved to death on a diet of self."[62]

As a pastor, you must preach and yearn for your students to be gripped by a vision for something more than their own comfort and convenience. Challenge them to serve and contribute in the church. Spark their imaginations by telling them about a mission trip they can join. If you want students to have a sense of significance, give them something significant to do together.

YOUR MOVE

It's time to reclaim the primacy of the sermon in youth ministry. We all know that playing games and having fun are both important. After all, if your students don't enjoy attending your church, they'll stop coming.

However, in the Great Commission, Jesus doesn't say, "Make them want to come back next week." He says, "Teach them to obey everything I have commanded you."

When you stand up to speak every week, you should have three objectives:

1. Describe God.

2. Expose the lies (and uncover the truth).

3. Empower students.

The sermon is central to your calling. It is part of your core brand. Don't let other things distract you from giving it the time and attention you know it deserves.

STRATEGY #22:

Don't underestimate the power of your sermons.

CHAPTER 23
PREACHING MISTAKES THAT NEW YOUTH PASTORS MAKE

You can spot him, can't you? The guy who tries really hard not to look nervous. The guy who sounds like the preachers he grew up listening to. The guy who crams too much information into one message.

You know the guy I'm talking about, don't you?

More often than not, that guy is a new youth pastor. Those are the mistakes that new youth pastors make because they haven't had a chance to get the repetitions that they need to get comfortable on stage yet.

Recently, I spent a few hours coaching a seminary student who was struggling with each of those things in his new position as a part-time youth pastor.

We talked a few times about his manuscript, and then I met him at his church to practice. He got on the stage and delivered the message to the empty room as if it were filled with students. I sat at the computer, listened, and clicked through the slides in ProPresenter. It's the kind of work that is uncomfortable, but incredibly valuable.

BE CONFIDENT

Right from the start, I could tell that he wasn't comfortable. He was fidgeting. He was pacing. He was talking way too fast. He was radiating a ton of nervous energy.

I stopped him and said, "If you aren't comfortable, your students won't be comfortable. You have to appear confident, not nervous."

"How do I appear confident?" he asked.

I gave him five pieces of advice:

1. DON'T ADMIT THAT YOU'RE NERVOUS.

We've all heard speakers fumble through some words at the start of their message and then say something like, "Sorry. I'm really nervous right now." It's an appeal for sympathy from the audience. The speaker knows he isn't off to a great start, and he wants to keep people from thinking less of him.

I agree with Garr Reynolds, a public speaking coach, who says, "The presentation is about the audience. Telling them how nervous you are does not serve their interest. Acknowledge to yourself that you are nervous – and that it is normal – but do not share this information with the audience."

You might feel nervous, but there's no need to admit it.

2. GET AN ANCHOR.

To keep from pacing all over the stage, I suggested that he grab onto the teaching table with the hand that was closest to it. That way, the table would act as an anchor to keep him from drifting all over the stage.

At key points in the message, he could walk to the other side of the table and grab on with the other hand.

3. FIND A FRIENDLY FACE.

In any crowd, there will be people who are interested in what you're saying and people who aren't interested in what you're saying. You can usually tell which is which by their body language.

Interested people will smile and nod as you make your points and tell your stories. Disinterested people look like they're ready to leave at any moment.

If you focus on the people who aren't interested in what you're saying, you'll feel like you aren't doing a good job. You'll begin to doubt your material or yourself. It will create a greater sense of nervousness. Instead, focus on the people who are interested. They'll give you a sense of reassurance, a sense that you've got this.

4. BELIEVE IN YOURSELF.

I'm convinced that we become nervous when we feel like we aren't adequate to meet the task at hand. We think that the moment is bigger than us. It's not true. You have to believe that you and your message are enough to meet these people at this moment.

5. STAND IN A POWER POSITION.

Power posing is a concept made popular by Amy Cuddy's TED Talk. She's a Harvard professor who found that positioning your body in certain ways actually increases your confidence. Nervous people try to limit their footprint. They shrivel up. They close off. They cross their arms. They put their hands in their pockets (not in a relaxed way).

One of the best ways to increase your confidence and decrease your nervousness, according to Cuddy, is to stand with your feet shoulder-width apart. Relax your shoulders and hold your head high. That's a classic power position. Open up your arms, like you're going to hug the audience. Those simple moves will release most of the anxiety you feel.

After that mini-lesson on overcoming nervousness, we moved forward to address a few other things.

WATCH YOUR TONE

The next thing I picked up on was his tone. It was strong, but too aggressive. His points felt more like accusations. It sounded like he'd listened to one too many John Piper sermons. Don't get me wrong; I think John Piper is an excellent preacher, but his style is *his* style. He has a doctorate and spent three decades at the same church. Not only that, but he speaks to adults, not middle school students.

I tried to explain to this guy that speaking like John Piper would alienate students, not attract them. I suggested, "Instead of casting yourself as a preacher, you'll do better to share your message as a caring friend or older brother. That will create a more conversational tone that the students will listen and respond to."

That suggestion helped him soften his tone and put him in a different frame of mind.

SHORTEN YOUR TALK

Next, we trimmed the amount of material in his talk. He was trying to do too much with one message. He had too many points and too many Bible verses. It was overwhelming.

We edited the talk down to one key point. We crafted a tweetable statement that would be the "Bottom Line" or "Big Idea." It was the one thing he wanted the students to remember, even if they didn't remember anything else. If they got that point, the message would be a success.

SHOW THE STORY

The last thing we did was create a story with slides. He had two screens in the room, one on either side of the stage. But he wasn't using them to help tell the story of his message. He had prepared a few slides for the Bible verses he wanted to use, but that was all.

As I listened to his talk and scrolled through the slides, I saw an opportunity to add to the story. In his talk, he mentioned that he was part of the marching band. I did a quick Google image search and added a picture of a marching band to show on the screens.

He talked about how a lanyard was a status symbol in his high school, so I added a picture of a lanyard.

He made a key statement that I thought was too important for the students to miss, so I created a slide with that statement on it.

Seth Godin is a provocative marketing expert who proposed something called The 200 Slide Solution. On his blog, he wrote, "The next time you find yourself on the hook for a 40-minute presentation (with slides!) consider, at least for a moment, a radical idea: A slide every 12 seconds. 200 slides in all…Slides create action."[63]

I don't think Godin's proposal is radical; I think it's right. Your students are visually stimulated. Slides help them see what you're talking about, and images communicate to them in ways that words alone can't.

We ended up with a message in which the slides didn't simply give information; they showed the story.

I was pleased to get this text message from him after I got home that night: "I learned more in a few hours from you today than I've learned all semester in my preaching class. Thank you so much!"

He's a new youth pastor, but he's on his way to speaking like a veteran.

YOUR MOVE

These mistakes aren't limited to just new youth pastors. Even experienced youth pastors can be nervous, use the wrong tone, speak too long, and fail to show the story. The important thing to remember is that all of these mistakes can be handled easily.

The rookie youth pastor that I met with was able to get these things sorted out with just a few hours of extra work. You can too.

STRATEGY #23:

Work hard to become a better speaker.

CHAPTER 24

THREE ASSUMPTIONS THAT CAN KILL YOUR SERMONS

Have you seen the television show called, "Adam Ruins Everything?" Adam Conover serves as the host who uses humor and logic to debunk long-standing assumptions about everything from how much water we should drink to why orange juice isn't really natural. It is really entertaining! And it proves the point that many of our assumptions are wrong.

WHAT ARE ASSUMPTIONS?

In *The Austere Academy* by Lemony Snicket, the narrator makes a keen observation about assumptions. He says, "Making assumptions simply means believing things are a certain way with little or no evidence that shows you are correct."

He goes on, "*Assumptions* are dangerous things to make, and like all dangerous things to make…if you make even the tiniest mistake you can find yourself in terrible trouble."[64]

It is necessary for us to make assumptions because they

keep us from having to use our limited mental energy to think through the same things we sorted out on previous occasions. When we make assumptions, we make unconscious predictions about the way things will go. Those predictions allow us to use our mental energy on new issues or challenges that demand our attention.

CHALLENGING YOUR ASSUMPTIONS

We all have assumptions that need to be challenged from time to time. For example, when my son was four years old, my wife and I tucked him into bed, said goodnight, and sat down to watch a movie in the living room. A few minutes later, my son came out of his room.

"I don't feel good," he said. I immediately assumed that he felt fine; he just didn't want to go to sleep. We paused the movie, and I walked him back to his room. A few minutes later, the scene repeated itself.

This time, however, after he announced that he didn't feel good, he threw up all over the floor! Clearly, my assumption was wrong.

One assumption that I often encounter when talking with youth pastors is that students should be able to sit still and absorb a 35-minute sermon. This assumption is well-intentioned. We love God, and we love talking, so it makes sense that we would want to talk about God for as long as we can.

Keep in mind, however, that even though your favorite preachers preach for forty minutes, they have two things going for them that you and I don't:

1. They are excellent at their craft (that's why they're your favorites).

2. They are speaking to adults.

Here's why those two things matter: You and I are still growing as speakers. Most of us haven't made it onto the list of anyone's favorite preachers. Not only that, we speak to students, not adults. So, I would recommend that you finish your sermons in less than twenty-five minutes. If TED Conference speakers can explain the complexities of neuroscience in eighteen minutes, it shouldn't take you much longer than that to talk about the Prodigal Son.

How about three more assumptions to avoid?

THREE ASSUMPTIONS
THAT CAN KILL YOUR SERMONS

ASSUMPTION #1:
STUDENTS *CARE* WHAT YOU'RE TALKING ABOUT.

In traditional churches, the pastor ascends to the podium, clears his throat, and announces his sermon text. At that point, the Scripture is read, and the sermon begins.

This approach assumes people care what the Bible says about a given topic. In my opinion, that is a faulty assumption today. Most of your students aren't sitting around wondering if their actions are acceptable to God. They aren't searching the Scriptures to see if their behavior aligns with God's design. For many, their desire to be cool is more important than their desire to be Christian.

Your fancy sermon titles and professional graphics might make you feel good, but they don't automatically make students care about the topic you're talking about. Instead, you have to spend time in your sermon creating a palpable tension that students want you to resolve.

Andy Stanley says it like this: "Assume no interest. Focus on the question you are intending to answer until you are confident your audience wants it answered. Otherwise you are about to spend twenty or thirty minutes of your life answering a question nobody is asking."[65]

Elsewhere, he says, "Before I draw people's attention to a solution, I want to make sure they are emotionally engaged with the problem."[66]

If you've watched any of his sermons, you know that part of Andy Stanley's appeal is that he assumes people don't care about his topic. His task, then, is to convince them that the topic has vital implications for their lives.

You have a similar task when it comes to your sermons. Don't assume students care just because they're there. Raise questions. Discuss issues. Create tension. Then – and only then – are you ready to move on to what the Bible has to say about your topic.

ASSUMPTION #2:
STUDENTS *KNOW* WHAT YOU'RE TALKING ABOUT.

I was playing basketball in the driveway with my son when a few kids from the neighborhood came over to join us. After a while, they got bored and wanted to play something else. They all went to my garage and saw random supplies for various games. They were pumped up about the possibilities!

In their excitement, they asked, "Why do you have all this stuff?"

"I'm a youth pastor," I said.

"What's a pastor?" they asked.

That was an eye-opener for me. Those kids ranged from

4th grade to 7th grade, but not one of them knew what a pastor was. One kid thought he might know. He said, "I think that's somebody who works at a church or something, right?"

These are the students that your students invite to your programs. They're the ones who show up at your church for the first time. That means that when you speak, you can't assume that everyone knows what you're talking about. They don't.

You have to define your terms more carefully. You can't just talk about God. Students will fill that idea up with their own presuppositions about who God is and what God is like. In a multi-cultural society, you have to clarify which God you're talking about and why it makes a difference.

You can't just mention the gospel, atonement, fellowship, or baptism and think that everyone in the room is on the same page. They're not. Half of them won't even know that Moses lived before Jesus.

Beware of saying things like, "You remember the story about Achan's sin in the book of Joshua, don't you?" They don't. Many of them have never even heard of it. You have to tell them. Explain everything.

Now, you might create thick tension to make students care. And you might even provide thorough explanations to help students understand what you're talking about, but there is still another assumption to consider.

ASSUMPTION #3:
STUDENTS *BELIEVE* WHAT YOU'RE TALKING ABOUT.

Beyond caring and knowing, there is the all-important factor of believing. Students who don't believe what you're saying will still show up to hear you say it. I remember showing up at Young Life club in high school. It was a Christian group, but I wasn't a Christian. I didn't believe what they were saying, but I went anyway.

Why did I keep showing up? I think I kept going for two reasons:

1. My friends were going.

2. The leaders let me proceed at my own pace.

The second reason is my focus here. When the Young Life leaders gave their talks each week, I got the sense that they believed what they were saying, even if I didn't.

What did I believe? I had no idea. But they didn't make me feel small or inferior because of my unbelief. They didn't threaten me with talk about hell. Instead, they gently challenged me by saying and showing that God wants what is best for me. That meant that God and I were on the same page; we were working toward the same goal. I was willing to believe that. And that was a good start.

Over time, it became clear that Jesus needed to become the Lord and Leader of my life, but it wasn't a quick conclusion. The leaders gave me space to sort it out. They were open and available to answer the questions that I had. They spoke in a way that left room for my doubts, while also making a convincing case for Christian faith.

The whole process reinforces what Andy Stanley says: "When people are convinced you want something FOR them rather than something FROM them, they are less likely to be offended when you challenge them."[67]

Don't assume students believe what you're talking about. In your sermons, your task is to give them reasons to believe by answering their questions in a way that shows Christianity is both intelligible and desirable.

YOUR MOVE

Assumptions are dangerous things to make. That should be evident every time you stand up to speak. Sermons are important in youth ministry, so it is important that you kill these assumptions before they have a chance to kill your sermons.

To summarize:

Don't assume students care what you're talking about. Create tension, raise the stakes, and help them see why they should care.

Don't assume students know what you're talking about. Tell them what you mean, explain everything, and aim for clarity.

Don't assume students believe what you're talking about. Inspire, equip, and empower them to find their own answers and discover their own faith.

STRATEGY #24:

Don't answer questions that your students aren't asking.

CHAPTER 25
THE FASTEST WAY TO PREACH BETTER SERMONS

Are you a better preacher than you were last year? Better yet, would your students say you're a better preacher than you were last year? If you're like most youth pastors, the answer is no. Why is that?

In his book, *So Good They Can't Ignore You*, Cal Newport explains, "If you just show up and work hard, you'll soon hit a performance plateau beyond which you fail to get any better."[68]

You show up. You work hard. But, if you're honest, you've hit a plateau. Your sermon content and delivery style are pretty much the same this year as they were last year.

It's a bit like bowling. Growing up, my parents took my brother and me to the bowling alley every Sunday morning. My dad even had his own ball and shoes. When we started this family tradition, I was pretty young, and we didn't use the bumpers to keep the ball from going into the gutter. My first scores were in the 50s.

It wasn't long, however, before I started to get the hang

of it. I consistently bowled my ball all the way down the lane and hit a few pins. Quickly, my score jumped up into the 80s. Eventually, my average would settle around 110. Even today, if I go to the bowling alley, I'm thrilled to get over 100.

But think about it. In the first several months, my average score went up by thirty points. Over the next three decades, my score has only gone up around twenty points from there. That's the phenomenon that Newport is describing. I hit a plateau.

But the real question is: How can you get off your own plateau and start preaching better sermons?

It's a good question.

RECORD YOURSELF

The fastest way to preach better sermons is to record yourself. This one insight will help you more than attending another webinar or reading another book about preaching.

I think we've all heard this advice somewhere along the way. What shocks me is how few of us actually do it. I think most people avoid recording themselves because there is something about hearing our own voices that makes us uncomfortable.

The first time I ever spoke at a church, they gave me a cassette tape of my message. My excitement turned to embarrassment when I listened. I talked too fast. I didn't make a clear point. There wasn't a solid call to action. It was bad. That was almost twenty years ago, but I still remember sitting there in my car thinking how awkward it was to listen to myself like that.

It's Not Just Awkward for Pastors

Famous singers know the feeling too. In an interview with BBC Radio, British singer Jessie J said, "I don't like listening to myself sing. It's weird listening to your own song. You'll be in Burger King or a theme park and you cringe."[69] Even Eric Clapton admitted, "I hate my singing. It all sounds like I'm 16 years old."[70]

I don't know the psychology behind it, but there's definitely something about hearing our own voices that makes us uncomfortable.

But that doesn't excuse us from listening. After all, if other people listen to us talk, then the least we can do is listen to what we're saying too. Plus, it is a necessary part of learning to preach better.

Recording Audio

At a minimum, you should make an audio recording of your message. Then, as painful as it might be, you have to listen to it.

This is easy for me because the soundboard at my church allows me to record directly to a USB drive. My car also has a USB port that allows me to play it through the stereo. If you don't have those fancy things, don't worry: all you really need is a phone with a voice recorder.

My habit is to listen to my sermon on the way home after church. I like to listen immediately after I speak because everything is still fresh in my mind at that point. I can still see myself saying those words. I can still see the students' faces when I told a certain story or explained part of a Bible verse. If I let a few days go by, then I'll lose that connection to the moment.

Sometimes, I find that I did better than I originally thought I did. Other times, I find that I wasn't as clear as I originally thought I was. Every time, I find something that I can do better next time.

RECORDING VIDEO

At my church, we record and evaluate everything that happens during the adult service. Everything.

On one of my first Sundays on staff, I was the one on the stage welcoming people and getting the service started. The next morning, I received an email containing the video file and a message asking me to evaluate myself.

Here are my actual comments from that self-evaluation:

1. Transitioned without a pause from welcome to the first announcement. *Action Step: Slow down.*

2. Probably shouldn't have said, "Hit it!" when the slide was supposed to change. *Action Step: Have fun, but remember the audience is primarily adults.*

3. Paced too much back and forth across the stage. *Action Step: Understand body language.*

4. Too many "uh's." *Action Step:* Practice replacing filler words. Space is okay.

If you thought the audio recording was harsh, video can be downright cruel! But it's necessary for getting better.

TJ Walker, CEO of Media Training Worldwide, says, "You have to see video of yourself speaking if you want to improve, and there is absolutely no excuse not to do so."[71]

The next time I was on stage, I did a lot better.

Again, this doesn't require high-tech video equipment.

You aren't filming for a professional movie; you're filming for your personal development. A simple flip camera or smart phone will work fine.

A FEW QUESTIONS

Here are a few questions you can ask yourself while you're watching your video:

1. Are you making eye contact?

2. Are you expressing emotion or are you monotone?

3. Are you enunciating your words so people can understand you?

4. How is your speed: Too fast? Too slow?

5. How is your volume: Too soft? Too loud?

6. How is your tone: Too passive? Too aggressive?

7. How is your body language: Nervous? Confident?

8. Are you using filler words (um, uh, etc.)?

9. If you were in the crowd, would you want to listen?

Once you have a good feel for how you look and sound, it's a good idea to continue with audio recordings every week and video recordings once every month.

YOUR MOVE

Just because you speak every week doesn't mean you're getting better at it. John Maxwell says, "Experience teaches nothing, but evaluated experience teaches everything."[72]

Recording yourself is one way to evaluate yourself as a

speaker, and it's the fastest way that I've found to start preaching better sermons.

STRATEGY #25:

Listen to yourself through the ears of your students.

CHAPTER 26
WHY STAFF MEETINGS STINK

If you have a bias toward action, then you probably loathe your weekly staff meetings. They sit there on your calendar, waiting to gobble up your precious time like Cookie Monster gobbles up cookies.

For those of you who have to prepare for multiple ministry programs every week, it's even worse. You need every minute you can get to make every distinct environment irresistible in its own right. The weekly staff meeting doesn't usually help in that effort.

Instead, it's like an armed intruder who shows up at your office to steal the one thing you can't replace: your time.

In his book, *Read This Before Our Next Meeting*, Al Pittampali says, "Traditional meetings seem to go on forever, with no end in sight. When the clock runs out, we add more time or, even worse, more meetings."[73]

It's not just a church problem. I spent five years working for a company that provided staffing support to the Department of Defense. Some weeks, it felt like we spent more time talking in meetings than actually working.

Don't get me wrong. It's not that meetings are completely worthless; they have value. It's just that many of our meetings are neither efficient nor productive.

MEETING STEW

The problem with typical weekly staff meetings is that they are scatterbrained. There's no agenda, and they try to cover too much information at one time. Instead of focusing on one or two specific items, assigning ownership, and determining next action steps and deadlines, they become what Patrick Lencioni calls "Meeting Stew."

What is Meeting Stew?

Lencioni explains: "Imagine a clueless cook taking all of the ingredients out of the pantry and the refrigerator and throwing them into one big pot, and then wondering why his concoction doesn't taste very good. Leaders do the same thing when they put all of the issues into one big discussion, usually called a 'staff meeting.'"[74]

That scene probably sounds familiar to you.

The way to have more productive meetings is counter-intuitive at first glance. That's because more productive meetings require you to have more meetings. But these are meetings of a different kind.

Instead of having one weekly, three-hour marathon meeting that includes everyone from the Nursery Coordinator to the Executive Pastor and everything from sermon series ideas to the quarterly church calendar, it is better to have more meetings with fewer people, smaller agendas, and shorter timeframes. The only people who need to be in a particular meeting are the key decision-makers or contributors for the issue that is being discussed.

For example, if you need ideas for an upcoming sermon series, hold a brainstorming meeting. Invite the most creative you know. If you need to discuss strategic initiatives for next year, then invite the people who think strategically or have vested interest in that discussion. If you feel like other staff members need to know what was discussed, then have someone write a meeting summary and send it to the people who weren't there.

If these kinds of meetings became the norm, Lencioni assures us, "Leaders actually come to look forward to their meetings, even enjoy them."[75]

BACK TO REALITY...

"That's great," you're probably thinking, "but I don't have any control over how often we meet, how long we meet, or even what we talk about when we meet."

For most of you – no matter what – next week your whole staff will gather around the table for another big bland helping of Meeting Stew.

I understand that. I've been there too. So, I want to suggest one simple way to get the most out of those meetings.

Here it is: *Prepare in advance.*

If your meetings are anything like the ones I was in, one of the most frustrating things is that people aren't prepared. Every week, they're asked to give a ministry update. But when it's their turn to share what is going on in their ministry, they mumble through it with predictable phrases like, "Things are going good."

Maybe you've been guilty of that. I know I was.

Eventually, I decided to prepare for that moment in the staff meeting when it was my turn to speak. I knew that

I would be asked for a ministry update, so I took thirty minutes before the meeting to collect my thoughts and jot down a few notes.

I focused on four timeframes:

1. This Week

2. Just Ahead (7-15 days out)

3. Around the Corner (16-30 days out)

4. Down the Road (31-90 days out)

For each timeframe, I listed four things:

1. Date

2. Action / Event

3. Concerns / Issues / Needs

4. Miscellaneous Notes

I remember when it was my turn to share. Instead of my usual blah, blah, blah, I moved systematically through my notes to explain specific details about what was coming up and where I needed help.

It was a satisfying feeling. I didn't feel like I had wasted my time in the meeting; it actually felt like I had made progress for my ministry. So, I did it again the next week. And again the week after that.

Eventually, I created a spreadsheet with the timeframes and categories that I thought were important. As the weeks rolled by, I would see things move from Down the Road to Around the Corner to Just Ahead to This Week.

If nothing else, it helped me stay on top of what was

happening in my ministry, so I wasn't scrambling at the last minute to put things together.

But it was more than that.

Because I was thinking ahead, I was able to enlist the help of other staff members. I was able to get items listed in the bulletin. I felt like I had a better grasp on what was happening in my ministry. Not only that, but I was also able to speak clearly about the good things happening within my ministry.

Staff meetings were still inefficient and sometimes counterproductive as a whole, but at least for those few minutes when I had the floor I felt like I had moved the ball down the field.

The best compliment came when our Children's Ministry Director asked me for a copy of my spreadsheet because she wanted to use it too.

YOUR MOVE

I doubt that your weekly staff meetings are going away any time soon. They will probably continue to be best described as Meeting Stew. But you can do your part to make that stew taste a little better.

Your meeting time will be wasted time if you don't take time to prepare for it. I have included my meeting preparation spreadsheet for you in the Bonus Material for this book. Print it out, and spend a few minutes before your next staff meeting to collect your thoughts and prepare your remarks.

You might not be able to change the entire structure of your meetings, but you can make them a little better by preparing in advance.

STRATEGY #26:

Make the most of your meetings by preparing in advance.

CHAPTER 27
WHY CHURCHES WON'T CHANGE

Whose fault is it when your church starts losing members? Whose fault is it when your youth ministry isn't adding students?

How you answer those questions says a lot about whether or not a declining church or plateaued ministry will be able to turn their situation around. You will either accept responsibility for your results, or you'll be like Curtis Gokey.

WHO IS CURTIS GOKEY?

In March of 2006, a city dump truck backed into Curtis Gokey's car. The car was damaged badly, so Gokey sued the city for the cost of repairs.

The catch? Curtis Gokey was driving the city dump truck that ran into his own personal car. He didn't want to take responsibility for the results he had created.[76]

Many churches are like that.

Many youth pastors are like that.

Although, I'm sure you're not one of them.

DON'T PLAY THE BLAME GAME

I worked at a church that didn't want to take responsibility for the results it had created. Attendance in the adult worship services had steadily declined for the last seven years. Student attendance had dropped too.

When I was hired, I asked about the reasons for the decline. I was given two answers:

1. The economic downturn.

2. Former staff members.

Whose fault was it that the church was losing members? They said it was the economy's fault. People didn't have enough money left over to give, therefore morale was low and people weren't attending.

Whose fault was it that the youth ministry wasn't adding students? They said it was the former youth pastor's fault. He talked down to students, so they didn't like him and didn't want to be involved anymore. The children's ministry was also stagnant, and the same excuse was being given for that.

Meanwhile, the parking lot was cracked, the building was falling apart, the décor was dated, the services were unimaginative, and money was being spent in irresponsible ways.

Weren't *those* things to blame for the decline? I thought they were, but others wanted to play the blame game.

It's not that the economy and the former staff members weren't factors; they were. The problem was that they were being blamed for all of the problems, while the church leadership accepted the responsibility for none of the problems.

What stood out to me in my conversations with other staff members and key leaders was the fact that no one was willing to accept responsibility for the current situation. Instead of accepting responsibility, they assigned blame.

They said that things went downhill when the economy went downhill. However, other churches in our area had grown and even gone through successful building programs in that same time period.

They said that former staff members had done irreparable damage. But who hired those people in the first place? The church did. More particularly, the church's leaders did.

Were those poorly performing staff members fired? No. Who kept those poorly performing staff members around to perpetuate the cycle of poor performance? The church did. More particularly, the church's leaders did.

No wonder the church was declining and the youth ministry was stuck.

It's Like the Rivers and the Sea

One of Aesop's Fables is called, "The Rivers and the Sea." Here's what it says:

"The rivers joined together to complain to the Sea, saying, 'Why is it that when we flow into your tides so potable and sweet, you work in us such a change, and make us salty and unfit to drink?' The Sea, perceiving that they intended to throw blame on him, said, 'Pray cease to flow into me, and then you will not be made briny.'"

The moral of the story: Don't blame others.

The Sea was simply doing what came naturally. If the rivers wanted to create a different result, then they should have done something different or found somewhere different to flow. Until then, however, the Sea would continue to turn the rivers into salty water that is unfit to drink. That's what it does.

The same thing is true for your church:

If you're losing people, then don't complain about what others are doing. Change what *you're* doing. If you aren't reaching new people, then don't criticize what others are doing. Change what *you're* doing.

Your system is perfectly designed to deliver the results you're currently getting. If you don't like your results, then change the system.

HOW THE MIGHTY FALL

In his book, *How the Mighty Fall*, researcher Jim Collins identifies five factors that lead to the decline, and eventual death, of an organization. Stage three in the downward slide is marked by "denial of risk and peril." Instead of accepting responsibility and adjusting their system, leaders blame external factors for their setbacks and continue with business-as-usual.[77]

This is an important lesson for church and ministry leaders. Before you can take the first step toward leading change, you have to accept responsibility for what has happened. Stop assigning blame; start accepting responsibility. Until that happens, your chances of changing are slim to none.

Your Move

Acknowledging the need for change requires people to admit that they have failed on some level. That is hard because sensitivities are high and egos can be large. Even so, the work of the church – and your ministry – is too important to suffer because we are afraid of having hard conversations.

A church in decline or a ministry that has plateaued should be ready for some candid conversations. Leaders should employ candor and openness as they talk about the way things are, as well as how they got to be that way. As long as those conversations are avoided, change will be an impossibility.

If your ministry is losing students, you need to ask why that's happening. Then you need to look in the mirror and ask what you can do differently to turn things around.

STRATEGY #27:

Accept responsibility for your results.

CHAPTER 28
HOW TO DEAL WITH DISCOURAGEMENT

You may recall this scene from *The Fellowship of the Ring*:

Frodo cries out, "I am not made for perilous quests. I wish I had never seen the Ring! Why did it come to me? Why was I chosen?"

Gandolf replies, "Such questions cannot be answered. You may be sure that it was not for any merit that others do not possess; not for power or wisdom, at any rate. But you have been chosen and you must therefore use such strength and heart and wits as you have."

Now, imagine this scene that feels a little closer to home:

A youth pastor named Brandon shows up at a new church with high hopes. He thinks to himself, "This church understands. This church is growing. This church has plenty of money in the budget! This church is so much better than the last church I was at."

He'd left his last church because he'd gotten discouraged. He felt like no one there really cared. They were just going through the motions. That church was losing members. How could he be expected to grow the youth ministry when the students' parents didn't even want to show up? As people left, the budget went from small to smaller.

Brandon went from discouraged to disillusioned and eventually started looking for another church to work at. Now he'd found one!

Three months go by. He hasn't made any changes because one of the longtime members told him that he'd better not change anything. He let Brandon know that the last youth pastor was loved by the students and the congregation. The only reason he'd left was to take a *real* job as a senior pastor somewhere.

Brandon takes the old man's advice; he doesn't change anything. But he feels disconnected from what he's doing. The Sunday morning program isn't as good as he thinks it can be. Wednesday nights are supposed to be the time when new students show up, but he hasn't seen a new student in six weeks. There were a few new students who came when the church announced they'd hired a new youth pastor, but none of them came back after that.

Brandon decides to make some changes. Immediately, the emails arrive in his inbox. He gets emails from parents who second-guess his plan. He gets emails from volunteers who balk at the increased demand the changes will require of them. He gets an email from the senior pastor that says, "I support you, Brandon, but you're on your own with these changes."

The support he'd hoped for wasn't coming through.

More time passes. Fewer students are showing up. Brandon begins to feel the dreaded feeling that he felt at his last church. It was the feeling of discouragement, again.

CHRONIC DISCOURAGEMENT

Brandon is not alone. Discouragement seems to be a constant battle in youth ministry. Doug Fields says, "When you say yes to ministry, you say yes to periods of discouragement. Anyone who doesn't admit to occasional seasons of discouragement owns a timeshare on Fantasy Island."[78]

Discouragement is what you feel when your expectations don't match reality. Maybe it's because so many of us are energetic, passionate, and a bit idealistic. Maybe it's because we really believe that God has gifted us to do something great. Whatever the reason, when we bring that passionate, energetic, idealism into a local church, we find out that the last three youth pastors were also energetic, passionate, and a bit idealistic before they left.

During your interview, they told you that those guys had outlandish ideas. They said that those guys just didn't understand how to do ministry in that setting. And you believed them.

You don't have outlandish ideas. You would figure out how to do ministry in that setting. So, you assumed you'd be a great fit. You took the job.

And now, here you are: discouraged. It could be six months or six years into the job. Either way, like an unwanted guest who shows up unannounced, discouragement has landed on your doorstep, and it plans to stick around for a while.

So, how do you deal with discouragement?

Here's how:

7 WAYS TO DEAL WITH DISCOURAGEMENT

1. TAKE A PERSONAL DAY

First of all, you have vacation days for a reason. According to a recent study, U.S. workers only use 77% of their paid time off.[79] Use of vacation days is at the lowest point in 40 years. Don't feel like you can only use your vacation days to go to the beach or to Disney World; use them for personal days off too.

Just like your cell phone battery loses its charge, you might just need to recharge for a day. What do you enjoy? Go out and spend a day doing that. It won't change anything about your ministry situation, but it will help you gain a more balanced perspective to think about what's really going on there. What you'll usually find is that things are seldom as good or as bad as they seem in the moment.

2. CONFIDE IN SOMEONE YOU TRUST

Being silent about your discouragement is the worst thing you can do with it. Your feelings won't go away when you suppress them; they'll get more intense. That's what living in denial does. Denial is when you refuse to acknowledge reality. Opening up with someone is the antidote to denial. And when you get your feelings out on the table, you can actually deal with them.

Don't broadcast your feelings across social media. That won't help. Instead, find someone you trust and talk to them. Through the years, I've been able to share my discouragement with guys who were successful in both business and church realms. My discouragement usually stems from a lack of results, so they understand where I'm coming from.

Right now, I have a friend who works at a church that is two hours north of mine. He's the kind of guy who always helps me gain perspective and clarity on situations. He cautions me from moving too fast and prods me when I'm moving too slow. His voice in my life is invaluable. You need someone like that.

Be very careful about confiding in someone who currently attends your church. I've heard more than one story of that backfiring because things went public that were meant to be kept private. Whoever you confide in, make sure they're trustworthy.

3. RECONNECT WITH GOD

Discouragement is often a symptom of being out of sync with God. That's not always the case, but it is often the case for the youth pastors I talk with. Ruth Haley Barton points out, "Many of us are choosing to live lives that do not set us up to pay attention, to notice those places where God is at work…We slide inexorably into a way of life that offers little or no opportunity for paying attention and then wonder why we are not hearing from God when we need God most."[80]

When was the last time you read the Bible because you enjoy it?

How often do you spend time in communion with God, enjoying his fellowship and presence?

In the Bonus Material for this chapter, I have included a document that will help you make the most of your time with God.

When you become disconnected from the source of ministry, don't be surprised if seasons of discouragement follow. I understand your discouragement might in fact stem from a holy discontent that you feel because you *are* close to God and you sense that he wants to do more in your ministry than you see happening in the present moment. But, more often than not, discouragement is a symptom of being out of sync with God.

When you're discouraged, it's time to lean on God.

4. Rediscover Your Calling

Frederick Beuchner says, "The place God calls you to is the place where your deep gladness and the world's deep hunger meet."[81] There was a time when you were convinced that you were called to youth ministry. Not only did you sense a call to youth ministry, you sensed a call to the church where you're currently serving.

It's easy to leave. Maybe you should leave. But don't rush to that decision, especially when you're discouraged.

Like Brandon in the story above, you might leave one discouraging situation only to find yourself in a new one. That's because people are still people no matter where you go. A guy told me one time that large churches and small churches both have problems; they just look different. I've worked at both small and large churches, and I can tell you that he was right.

To rediscover your calling, you need to think about the things you've accomplished so far in your ministry. I'm not talking about a vague thought that you've impacted a bunch of students. I want you to name them:

- Kara became a Christian because of this ministry.
- Sean developed the confidence to share his faith with his friends.
- Samantha prayed out loud in a group for the first time.

- Derek was baptized because of this ministry.
- Ryan is a leader at his college because I mentored him two years ago.

Os Guiness says, "Calling is the truth that God calls us to himself so decisively that everything we are, everything we do, and everything we have is invested with a special devotion, dynamism, and direction lived out as a response to his summons and service."[82]

When it comes to your calling, there will always be times of success and times of struggle. They go together. That's how it is. You have to remember that seasons of discouragement don't take away from your seasons of encouragement. When you're tempted to leave, you should consider that perhaps your work isn't done yet. You might be on the brink of a breakthrough.

5. RETHINK YOUR EXPECTATIONS

It's possible that you need to rethink your expectations. You might have had dreams of growing your ministry so large that you needed to build a new student building. But that might not be the situation you're actually in.

Instead of complaining to the nine students who consistently come about the nineteen students who don't, what if you changed the scoreboard? What if you took the long view instead of the short view?

Instead of making weekly attendance your key metric, what if you measured the number of community service hours your students perform instead? Or what if your goal was that every student in your ministry serves in another ministry in your church? Or maybe your goal could be that every middle student reads through the whole New Testament before high school. And then that every high school student reads through the whole Bible before they graduate.

If discouragement comes from expectations that don't match reality, then why not change your expectations?

Don't let me or anyone else tell you what success should look like in your ministry. Your church hired you because they believe that you know what it takes to get the job done in your specific setting. Don't play the comparison game. Different churches have different cultures, and you have to make the most of the ministry you have.

If growth isn't a reasonable expectation, then change it to something that *is* reasonable and your discouragement will go away.

6. Create an Encouragement File

Every time a parent, volunteer, or student sends me an encouraging note, email, or text message, I save it in an encouragement file. For me, that file is just a note in my iPhone. I keep copying and pasting those messages into that one, long note.

The latest entry came as a text message from a student's mom. Here's what she said:

> *"Caleb told me that he ate lunch with you today. I know you didn't have to go eat lunch with him, but I believe God used you to brighten his day. He really thinks a lot of you and the first thing he told me after school was that he ate lunch with you. Thank you for all you do to make a difference."*

It's hard to look through a long list of notes like that and stay discouraged. Start keeping those encouraging notes and look back at them when you're feeling discouraged. They'll help you turn things around.

7. GET BACK TO WORK

I think the worst thing you can do when you're discouraged is sit and stew about it. It's not healthy. Besides that, it's not productive and doesn't help you move forward. The thing that *will* help you move forward is going to work and getting things done. Achievement builds confidence, which creates encouragement.

Can you imagine one of your volunteers moping around at their job because someone hurt their feelings or because they just don't feel passionate about it anymore? Of course not. Neither should you! You're a pastor, but you're also a professional. You're an employee of the church.

In his book, *The War of Art,* Steven Pressfield contrasts the professional and the amateur. In essence, the amateur shows up when it's fun and convenient. The professional shows up when it's neither fun nor convenient.

I'll be honest. I think we have a lot of amateurs in youth ministry. They're the guys who get into this work because they thought it was going to be like a permanent summer camp. They're the ones who get discouraged and quit when they find out that it's not like that at all.

But I know that's not you.

You're a pro. You're in it for the long haul. So, work these steps and get back to the office. You've got a job to do.

YOUR MOVE

Discouragement is like an unwanted guest who shows up unannounced at your doorstep and plans to stick around for a while. Don't let it in. And if it's already gotten in, then you need to treat it like it's a 30-year-old guy who still lives in his parents' basement: kick it out as soon as possible.

When you find yourself feeling discouraged, start at step one and then move through the rest of the list as you need it.

Step 1: Take a personal day.

Step 2: Confide in someone you trust.

Step 3: Reconnect with God.

Step 4: Rediscover your calling.

Step 5: Rethink your expectations.

Step 6: Create an encouragement file.

Step 7: Get back to work.

STRATEGY #28:

Don't let discouragement take you down.

CHAPTER 29

RECOVERING THE LOST ART OF SABBATH

Our pace of life is getting faster and faster. Computers, the internet, and smart phones have all contributed to that.

I remember getting on the internet for the first time in 1997. I was in 10th grade. Students today can't even imagine the world without the internet. They're Digital Natives.

I didn't even have a cell phone until I got to college. And all that I could do on it was call people!

Then came iPods. What started off as 1,000 songs in your pocket has become the whole world in your pocket. I remember having to do a report about astronauts when I was in middle school. You can probably guess what I did. I went to my family's collection of World Book Encyclopedias and pulled out the "A" volume.

If you type "astronauts" into the Google search form today, you'll get 25 million results back in half of a second.

Everything is getting faster.

Even family dinners are getting faster. Think about this: In 1950, the average dinnertime was ninety minutes. Can you imagine that? Today, the average dinnertime is twelve minutes.

One recent study found that 10% of families eat dinner together only one time each week. Between kids' activities, homework, and crazy work schedules for both parents, it seems that families don't have any family time anymore.[83]

Everything is moving faster than it did before.

THE FOURTH COMMANDMENT

The fourth of the Ten Commandments addresses this topic head-on. It says, "Remember the Sabbath day by keeping it holy" (Exodus 20:8 NLT).

Sabbath is a Hebrew word that means "to stop." Stop working. Stop going. Stop striving. Stop everything. There was one day in their weekly rhythm where the Jewish people just stopped.

Because things are moving so fast, it's hard for us to fathom such an idea. We want to get ahead. We want to go. We want to do. We don't want to miss out. We don't want to be left out.

But you know as well as I do that there are times when you just need to stop.

Pause.

Take a breath.

Remember why you're here.

Remember what you're doing.

Remember what it's all about.

Remember why it matters.

It's like God saw that life naturally pulls us toward getting more, doing more, achieving more. And he says there's a different way.

Look at the people around you. Look at the pace of their lives. They're frantic and frazzled. They're anxious, greedy, and selfish. God says there's a better way.

"Remember the Sabbath day by keeping it holy."

Yes, but what – specifically – is Sabbath for?

SABBATH IS FOR FOUR THINGS

1. SABBATH IS FOR REST

In the Exodus account, the reason you should take a Sabbath is because God did. God did his work in six days and then rested. That's what you should do too. I love what Eugene Peterson says: "If we do not regularly quit work for one day a week we take ourselves too seriously."[84]

Rest isn't just theological; it's also practical. Your mind and body are stronger when you take time off. You feel better. Your relationships are better. Rest is essential to your life, and recovering the Sabbath ensures that you will get the rest you need.

2. SABBATH IS FOR REFLECTION

Reflection is about looking back at the week gone by, and looking forward to the week ahead.

When you look back, you think about last week:

What was the best part?

What was the worst part?

What would you do differently next time?

Experience doesn't make you wiser; evaluated experience makes you wiser. When you look back, you evaluate your experiences so you can learn, grow, and keep from making the mistakes twice.

When you look ahead, you think about next week:

What do you need to prepare for?

What are you excited about?

What are your goals?

There's an old saying: Proper planning prevents poor performance. If you want to perform well in the coming week, take the time to plan and get prepared for what's ahead.

3. Sabbath Is for Relationships

Just like reflection, relationships have two prongs: with God and with others.

a. With God. When life gets hectic, it's easy to leave God out of the picture. That's a mistake that I'm sure you don't intend to make. But lots of youth pastors make it. Devotional time with God is replaced by sermon preparation time. Prayer time gets stolen away by another meeting. You know how it goes.

You need a day set aside each week where you really focus on connecting with God. You need to sing. You need to be taught. You need to be encouraged.

If you aren't able to do that at your own church, then find another church that meets at a different time and go there. If you can't find another church, then attend another church's online campus.

Do whatever it takes to keep your relationship with God fresh. Actively seek out ways to re-center your focus and priorities around God.

b. With Others. You need friends. You were made for community. When things get busy, it's easy to push other people away. It's easy to hunker down and start binge-watching shows on Netflix. That's why pastoral loneliness is a major problem today.

You need to fight the urge to become secluded. Find ways to connect with other youth pastors. Reach out to an older pastor in your area and ask him to meet with you. You don't need an agenda. Just meet together to build the relationship and reinforce your common calling to serve the body of Christ.

Don't underestimate the importance of like-minded people who can help you on your own journey of faith. You're pouring into students; make sure you have someone who is pouring into you.

5. Sabbath Is for Resistance.

This is the part of Sabbath that I didn't appreciate until recently. An Old Testament scholar named Walter Brueg-gemann helped me see it. He says, "Sabbath – actual, concrete, visible, regular discipleship – is a sign. It signifies an alternative life."[85]

When the Israelites received the Fourth Commandment, they had just come out of Egypt. They had worked in a culture that gave no time off. Pharaoh demanded ever-increasing quotas of bricks. When they met their quotas, they were given higher quotas. No amount was ever enough.

God told the Israelites that it would be different with him in charge. They were to stop working. They were to trust him and depend on him. Six days they could work, but on the seventh day they were told to resist.

When we stop working, stop going, and stop striving, we actively resist the popular culture that ties our worth to our production and performance. By saying yes to Sabbath, we're saying no to that culture and its demands.

Your Move

In a world that keeps getting faster and faster, we must be intentional about slowing down. God calls us to a different way, a better way. It is the Sabbath way of rest, reflection, relationships, and resistance.

STRATEGY #29:

Slow down before you burn out.

CHAPTER 30
MY SIX BIGGEST MISTAKES
(AND WHAT I LEARNED FROM THEM)

Everyone makes mistakes. You've made them. I've made them. We've all made them. Mistakes aren't bad unless you don't learn from them. The goal isn't mistake-free youth ministry; it's better youth ministry. However, if you make the same mistake over and over, don't be surprised if you find yourself called into the pastor's office to discuss your future at the church.

One mistake that I'll never make again is using regular shampoo for a slip and slide. When I was a new youth pastor, I had a great idea for a Water Day. We had water balloons, water guns, and all kinds of water-themed activities.

One of those activities was a slip and slide. I doused the tarp in shampoo and encouraged the students to dive on. The first student to try was the pastor's daughter. She ran fast and dove. She slid the whole way. It was great; it worked! But then she started screaming, "My eyes are burning! My eyes are burning!"

I learned a valuable lesson that day:

If you're going to do a slip and slide, you'd better use baby shampoo.

I wish that were the only mistake I've made, but it's not. In fact, it doesn't even make it on the list of the six biggest mistakes I've made in youth ministry.

What's on the list?

Here it is…

MY 6 BIGGEST MISTAKES IN YOUTH MINISTRY

MISTAKE #1:
I FORCED CHANGES.

I had just become a youth pastor, so I did what every youth pastor did back then: I read *Purpose Driven Youth Ministry* by Doug Fields. That book explains how programs should have specific audiences in mind. For example, your outreach program will have a different agenda than your student leadership program because they are intended for different groups. That makes sense.

What doesn't make sense is how I applied that information. (For the record, this mistake is not Doug Fields' fault.) I decided that our Wednesday night program would be reserved for student leaders. The only students who were allowed to attend were those who had gone through our Student Leadership 101 class. Other students would show up on Wednesday nights, and I would turn them away because the program wasn't designed for them.

I can't even believe it as I'm telling this story! It was a huge mistake (obviously!). Granted, I had no idea what I was really doing; I just thought I was applying what the book had said to do. But I was applying it in the wrong way.

After three weeks, I was asked to attend a meeting with the deacons of the church to explain what I had done. Let's just say it didn't go well for me. We opened Wednesday nights back up to any students who wanted to attend.

I could have spared myself the embarrassment of that mistake by asking for input from key leaders before implementing new ideas on my own.

LESSON #1: Ask for input from key leaders.

MISTAKE #2:
I KEPT BAD VOLUNTEERS TOO LONG.

It's not hard to make a difference as a volunteer in youth ministry. If someone will show up consistently, have a positive attitude, care about students, and point them to Jesus, they'll do great. And yet, people will volunteer to work with students who can't seem to get those things right. I've had lots of people like that in my ministries through the years.

In the early days, I would keep those people on the team. I was afraid I wouldn't have anyone else to fill their spot. But seriously, they weren't even filling their own spot in the first place! Every week I would wonder if they would show up. When they did show up, they had a bad attitude. They weren't prepared. They talked to everyone except for the students they were supposed to be leading.

And yet, I kept them around. I guess I thought they'd eventually get it. I figured they couldn't be *that* bad for *that* long. But they never got it. The students under their care grew disinterested and eventually stopped attending.

I should have dismissed those volunteers after three strikes. Your ministry is too important to leave in the hands of people who aren't passionate about students.

LESSON #2: Don't be afraid to dismiss underperforming volunteers.

MISTAKE #3:
I DIDN'T PARTNER WITH PARENTS.

In my early days, I imagined youth ministry as a partnership between my students and me. I didn't understand or emphasize the role of parents in the equation. Don't get me wrong; I never talked badly about parents; I just never considered them to be very important for my ministry.

Along came Reggie Joiner. He had a bright idea. When you mix the heart of parents (red) and the light of the church (yellow), you get orange. So, he wrote a book called, *Think Orange.* In that book, Joiner unpacks what he calls the 3,000/40 Principle. Basically, in a given year the church has approximately forty hours with a student. In that same year, their parents have approximately three thousand hours with them. It's a big mistake not to partner with parents. In Joiner's words, "It's your mission to help every parent win."[86]

Here are three simple ways to partner with parents:

a. Meet and Greet. Host a breakfast for parents and small group leaders to meet each other.

b. Monthly Emails. Send monthly emails to tell parents what you're teaching at church, and give them tips for creating discussions around those topics at home.

c. Helpful Resources. Parents want your help. Send them

information that will help them understand their teenager better. Send them tools to help them celebrate milestones together.

In the Bonus Material, I've included a resource for you to help parents commemorate their student's 13th birthday. It's called the "13th Birthday Blessing." It's one of the most helpful, meaningful things I've ever given to parents.

When you help parents win, you help students win.

LESSON #3: Find ways to partner with parents and help them win.

MISTAKE #4:
I DIDN'T LEARN ABOUT THE CHURCH.

I went through a long interview process with a church, but it was one-sided. They interviewed me, but I didn't interview them. I still remember getting the phone call when they offered me the job. I accepted it on the spot; no questions asked.

When I started working there, however, I started noticing some things. When I noticed things, I asked questions, and the answers I received weren't very promising.

Apparently, the church was in a tough spot financially. During the interview process, I should have asked if the church was meeting their annual budget and how that budget has changed over the last five years.

They had also experienced a lot of staff turnover. During the interview process, I should have asked about the staff tenure. Who has been there the longest? Who is the newest? How many staff members have left in the last three years?

Because the church's attendance was higher than the church I was coming from, I assumed everything was good. It didn't occur to me that even though more people attended the new church, total attendance there could still be in decline, which it was. Because of that, I learned to ask about attendance trends for the previous two years.

The interview process gave the church a chance to get to know me, but I didn't use that time to get to know the church.

LESSON #4: Find out all you can about the church before you say yes.

MISTAKE #5:
I PLAYED THE COMPARISON GAME.

In a classic case of learning that doesn't translate into action, this was a mistake that I shouldn't have made. Doug Fields warns new youth pastors to steer clear of the comparison game. He says, "When you compare you lose. Either you're filled with pride because you're better than another person, or you're dejected because you don't measure up."[87]

I was on the side of dejection. Other churches in town had more resources and more students than we did. I doubted my skills, my calling, and myself. Looking back, I see how misguided I was. At the time, however, I felt like I didn't measure up.

That's how the comparison game works: you're faithful, efficient, and effective in your own church (the place to which God has called you), but you still keep an eye on what everyone else has and what everyone else is doing.

Watching what others are doing isn't bad; it's an important

way to learn. It turns bad when you compare what you have and what you're doing to what they have and what they're doing.

When you compare, you lose.

LESSON #5: Learn from others, but don't compare yourself to them.

MISTAKE #6:
I DIDN'T ESTABLISH PERSONAL BOUNDARIES.

In their book, *Boundaries,* Henry Cloud and John Townsend define boundaries as "anything that helps to differentiate you from someone else, or show where you begin and end."[88]

I was newly married when I was hired as a full-time youth pastor. I had no idea how to balance being a husband with being a youth pastor. Students would come to my house almost every night of the week. That made it especially hard to spend quality time with my wife. If students weren't coming over, then I'd be out at their games. I would get home, and all the lights were out because my wife was already asleep.

I had no boundaries. Our marriage was strained, and I started to blame ministry for our struggles. In retrospect, I was the one to blame. I didn't establish personal boundaries to ensure healthy ministry.

If I had it to do over again, I would set aside specific nights for my family. These would be non-negotiable. No students. No ministry. Just family.

LESSON #6: Set aside specific time for your family.

YOUR MOVE

There are two kinds of examples. Some examples show you what to do. Others show you what not to do. I have shared with you the mistakes that I made. These are examples of what not to do.

I wish I knew better, but I didn't. You can either learn the easy way or the hard way. It's up to you. You can learn from my mistakes. That would be the easy way. Or, if you don't learn from my mistakes, then you'll have to learn the hard way with mistakes of your own. You don't need to do that.

STRATEGY #30:

Learn from your mistakes.

CONCLUSION
WHAT IS THE PURPOSE OF YOUTH MINISTRY?

What is the purpose of youth ministry?

Purpose, according to the Cambridge Dictionary, is an intention or aim; a reason for doing something. So, to rephrase the question, what is the reason for doing youth ministry? What is its aim?

If you were to ask ten different youth pastors, you would probably get ten different answers. Many times, those answers would be delivered in grandiose mission statements that are so long no one can remember them. However, if you cut away the catch-phrases and buzzwords, answers about the purpose of youth ministry usually range from reaching students to retaining them, and from educating students to entertaining them.

If there's any doubt how you would answer the question about the purpose of youth ministry, just look at your calendar, budget, and message transcripts. Your answer will be obvious.

After spending well over a decade in youth ministry, I

am convinced that the purpose of youth ministry is faith formation through participation.

This answer, with its twin emphasis on formation and participation, keeps us from the false dichotomies that say you have to choose between reaching or retaining and educating or entertaining.

The problem with those choices is that they're not mutually exclusive. It's possible to reach new students while at the same time retaining the ones who already attend. It's possible to educate students about the faith while at the same time making it entertaining for them.

The concept of faith formation picks up on these possibilities. You have to add students and keep them. You have to educate them and make it worth their time. It's all important. But, most importantly, "formation" captures the unfinished, developing nature of faith – especially in teenagers. Students are a work in process. Who they are today is not who they will be tomorrow.

This formation happens through participation. The concept of participation brings together all of the various pieces of experiential learning that are vital for growing faith in teenagers. So, more specifically, I see participation as instruction, action, reflection, and conversation.

Participation happens as you teach students the biblical story of God's active presence in the world. Action happens as you coordinate activities that allow students to participate in that story. Reflection happens as you open spaces for students to think about what they've seen and heard along the way. And conversation happens as you offer venues for students to talk about what they think and believe so they can move forward.

If the purpose of youth ministry is faith formation through participation, then your job is to create environments, plan activities, open spaces, and offer venues that work together toward that end.

My hope is that these thirty strategies will help you do that.

And here's one last strategy for you:

Remember that every week matters.

WRAP UP
SUMMARY OF THE STRATEGIES

STRATEGY #1:

Stay close to God.

STRATEGY #2:

Keep watch over your head, heart, and hands.

STRATEGY #3:

Invite others to evaluate your leadership abilities.

STRATEGY #4:

Get serious about personal growth.

STRATEGY #5:

Increase your likeability factor.

STRATEGY #6:

Make the hard choices.

STRATEGY #7:

Make the most of your dollars and cents.

STRATEGY #8:

Identify and achieve your strategic initiatives.

STRATEGY #9:

Help people see, experience, and remember your vision.

STRATEGY #10:

Give your volunteers what they really want.

STRATEGY #11:

Build a high-performance volunteer team.

STRATEGY #12:

Clarify the win for your small group leaders.

STRATEGY #13:

Do everything you can
to get your volunteers more involved.

STRATEGY #14:

Organize your schedule around your strengths.

STRATEGY #15:

Accomplish more by doing less.

STRATEGY #16:

Help students express their worship through singing.

STRATEGY #17:

Make students say "Wow!"

STRATEGY #18:

Take time to think about what happened and why.

STRATEGY #19:

Follow up with every student who attends your ministry.

STRATEGY #20:

Create a space where students want to meet.

STRATEGY #21:

Show students how much you care.

STRATEGY #22:

Don't underestimate the power of your sermons.

STRATEGY #23:

Work hard to become a better speaker.

STRATEGY #24:

Don't answer questions that your students aren't asking.

STRATEGY #25:

Listen to yourself through the ears of your students.

STRATEGY #26:

Make the most of your meetings by preparing in advance.

STRATEGY #27:

Accept responsibility for your results.

STRATEGY #28:

Don't let discouragement take you down.

STRATEGY #29:

Slow down before you burn out.

STRATEGY #30:

Learn from your mistakes.

BONUS STRATEGY:

Remember that every week matters.

DID YOU ENJOY THIS BOOK?

I want to thank you for purchasing and reading this book. I really hope you got a lot out of it.

Can I ask you to do me a quick favor?

If you enjoyed this book, I would really appreciate a positive review on Amazon. I love getting feedback, and reviews really do make a difference.

I read all of my reviews and would really appreciate your thoughts.

You can also connect with me on Twitter at @betteryouthmin

Thank you!

DOWNLOAD YOUR FREE BONUS MATERIAL

To say thank you for your purchase, I'd like to send you the FREE Bonus Material that goes along with this book. It includes dozens of templates and tools to help you create momentum, reach students, and grow faith in your ministry.

Download your FREE Bonus Material at:

www.betteryouthministry.com/everyweekmatters

LOOKING FOR ONE ON ONE COACHING?

I can help your ministry gain momentum and get results. Here are some of the ways I can help:

RESOURCES

From administrative templates to games to message series, I can connect you with tools that will immediately take your ministry to the next level.

STRATEGY

Some things create more impact and more results than others. I can help you discover what's holding you back and how to move forward.

VOLUNTEER TRAINING

Your ministry will only be as good as the leaders around you. I can help you recruit, train, and inspire your volunteers.

PERSONAL DEVELOPMENT

You are a combination of the books you read, the people you spend time with, and the podcasts you listen to. I can point you in the right direction.

COMMUNICATION

How you say what you say is important. I can help you craft compelling messages that get students to respond.

Learn more at:

www.betteryouthministry.com/coaching

ABOUT THE AUTHOR

Trevor Hamaker helps youth pastors do ministry better. He has over a decade of youth ministry experience, along with degrees in business management, organizational leadership, and religious education. Find out more at betteryouthministry.com.

MORE BOOKS BY TREVOR HAMAKER

People Skills for Youth Pastors: 33 Ways to Meet More People and Make a Bigger Difference in Youth Ministry

Your First 90 Days in a New Youth Ministry: A Simple Plan for Starting Right

Building a Better Youth Ministry: 30 Ways in 30 Days

Varsity Faith: A Thoughtful, Humble, Intentional, and Hopeful Option for Christian Students

END NOTES

1   Alvin L. Reid, *Raising the Bar: Ministry to Youth in the New Millennium* (Grand Rapids, MI: Kregel, 2004), 17.

2   Matt Woodley, "Catalyst 2011 Final Message with Andy Stanley." Online: http://www.christianitytoday.com/pastors/2011/october-online-only/catalyst-2011-final-message-with-andy-stanley.html (accessed 26 December 2016).

3   Charles Duhigg, *The Power of Habit: Why We Do What We Do in Life and Business* (New York, NY: Random House, 2012), 101.

4   John Ortberg, *Soul Keeping: Caring for the Most Important Part of You* (Grand Rapids, MI: Zondervan, 2014), 14.

5   Andy Stanley, *Like a Rock: Becoming a Person of Character* (Nashville, TN: Thomas Nelson, 1997), 25.

6   Ibid., 29.

7   Dallas Willard, "Why It Matters If You Are Moral." Online: http://www.dwillard.org/articles/artview.asp?artID=121 (accessed 28 December 2016).

8   Andy Stanley, *The Next Generation Leader: 5 Essentials for Those Who Will Shape the Future* (Colorado Springs, CO: Multnomah Books, 2003), 152.

9   C. S. Lewis, *Mere Christianity* (New York, NY: Touchstone, 1996), 87.

10 H. B. London, Jr. and Neil B. Wiseman, *Pastors at Greater Risk* (Grand Rapids, MI: Baker Books, 2003).

11 Wayne Cordeiro, *Leading on Empty: Refilling Your Tank and Renewing Your Passion* (Bloomington, MN: Bethany House, 2009), 33.

12 Tony Morgan and Tim Stevens, *Simply Strategic Volunteers: Empowering People for Ministry* (Loveland, CO: Group Publishing, 2005), 47.

13 James M. Kouzes and Barry Z. Posner, *The Leadership Challenge*, 4th ed. (San Francisco, CA: Jossey-Bass, 2007), 32.

14 Ibid., 33.

15 Ibid., 34.

16 Ibid., 35.

17 Ibid., 38.

18 Ken Blanchard and Mark Miller, *Great Leaders Grow: Becoming a Leader for Life* (San Francisco, CA: Berrett-Koehler Publishers, 2012), 33-34.

19 Ibid., 78.

20 Ibid., 100.

21 Ibid., 116.

22 Tim Sanders, *The Likeability Factor: How to Boost Your L-Factor and Achieve Your Life's Dreams* (New York, NY: Three Rivers Press, 2006), 33.

23 Michael Lovas and Pam Holloway, *Axis of Influence: How Credibility and Likeability Intersect to Drive Success* (Garden City, NY: Morgan James, 2009), 6.

24 Karen Friedman, *Shut and Say Something: Business Communication Strategies to Overcome Challenges and Influence Listeners* (Santa Barbara, CA: Praeger, 2010), 132.

25 John C. Maxwell and Les Parrott, *25 Ways to Win with People: How to Make Others Feel Like a Million Bucks* (Nashville, TN: Thomas Nelson, 2005), 34-35.

26 David Schwartz, *The Magic of Thinking Big,* reprint ed. (New York, NY: Touchstone, 2015), 211.

27 Art Anthony, "5 Small Decisions With Surprising Consequences." Online: http://www.therichest.com/rich-list/the-biggest/5-small-decisions-with-surprisingly-huge-costs/ (accessed 28 December 2016).

28 Marcus Buckingham, *The Truth About You: Your Secret to Success* (Nashville, TN: Thomas Nelson, 2008), 85.

29 Peter Greer and Chris Horst, *Mission Drift: The Unspoken Crisis Facing Leaders, Charities, and Churches* (Minneapolis, MN: Bethany House, 2014), 18, 20.

30 Ibid., 27.

31 George Barna, *Turning Vision Into Action* (Ventura, CA: Regal Books, 1996), 10.

32 Rick Warren, *The Purpose Driven Church: Growth Without Compromising Your Message and Mission* (Grand Rapids, MI: Zondervan, 1995), 111.

33 Andy Stanley, *Visioneering* (Sisters, OR: Multnomah, 1999), 202.

34 Ibid., 205.

35 Ibid., 210.

36 Ibid., 214.

37 Andy Stanley, *Making Vision Stick* (Grand Rapids, MI: Zondervan, 2007), 19.

38 Ibid., 24.

39 Ibid., 38.

40 Ibid., 39.

41 Ibid., 47.

42 Andy Stanley, *Deep and Wide: Creating Churches Unchurched People Love to Attend* (Grand Rapids, MI: Zondervan, 2012), 130.

43 Mark Miller, *The Secret of Teams: What Great Teams Know and Do* (San Francisco, CA: Berrett-Koehler Publishers, 2011), 75.

44 Rodd Wagner and James K. Harter, *12: The Elements of Great Managing* (New York, NY: Gallup Press, 2006), 23.

45 Danny Griffiths, "Confused Basketball Player Scores Last-Minute Goal in Wrong Net." Online: http://metro.co.uk/2013/03/08/confused-basketball-player-scores-last-minute-goal-in-the-wrong-net-3532622/ (accessed 29 December 2016).

46 Simon Sinek, *Start with Why: How Great Leaders Inspire Everyone to Take Action* (New York, NY: Penguin Group, 2009), 39.

47 Andy Stanley, Reggie Joiner, and Lane Jones, *7 Practices of Effective Ministry* (Sisters, OR: Multnomah, 2004), 72.

48 Stanley, *Making Vision Stick*, 40-41.

49 Stanley, *The Next Generation Leader*, 18.

50 Marcus Buckingham, *Go Put Your Strengths to Work: 6 Powerful Steps to Achieve Outstanding Performance* (New York, NY: Free Press, 2007), 85.

51 Stanley, *The Next Generation Leader*, 18-19.

52 Stanley, Joiner, and Jones, *7 Practices*, 102.

53 Ibid., 106.

54 Marc Lillibridge, "A Former Player's Perspective on Film Study and Preparing for an NFL Game." Online: http://bleacherreport.com/articles/1427449-a-former-players-perspective-on-film-study-and-preparing-for-a-nfl-game# (accessed 1 January 2017).

55 Ibid.

56 Charles Spurgeon, *Lectures to My Students* (Grand Rapids, MI: Zondervan, 1956), 129.

57 Tim Cool, *Why Church Buildings Matter: The Story of Your Space* (Nashville, TN: Rainer Publishing, 2013), 104.

58 Doug Fields, *Your First Two Years in Youth Ministry: A Personal and Practical Guide to Starting Right* (Grand Rapids, MI: Zondervan, 2002), 84.

59 Steven Davidoff Solomon, "A History of Misses for RadioShack." Online: http://dealbook.nytimes.com/2014/09/16/for-radioshack-a-history-of-misses/?_r=0 (accessed 1 January 2017).

60 Ibid.

61 Lewis, *Mere Christianity*, 54.

62 Eugene Peterson, *Christ Plays in Ten Thousand Places: A Conversation in Spiritual Theology* (Grand Rapids, MI: Wm. B. Eerdmans, 2005), 243.

63 Seth Godin, "The 200 Slide Solution." Online: http://sethgodin.typepad.com/seths_blog/2010/07/the-200-slide-solution.html (accessed 1 January 2017).

64 Lemony Snicket, *The Austere Academy* (New York, NY: HarperCollins, 2000), 187.

65 Stanley and Jones, *Communicating for a Change*, 125.

66 Stanley, *Deep and Wide*, 240.

67 Ibid., 245.

68 Cal C. Newport, *So Good They Can't Ignore You: Why Skills Trump Passion in the Quest for Work You Love* (New York, NY: Hachette, 2012), 85.

69 Huffington Post, "Jessie J's Music: British Singer Doesn't Like Listening To Her Own Songs." Online: http://www.huffingtonpost.com/2013/06/03/jessie-j-music-doesnt-like-listening-to-her-own-songs_n_3377745.html (accessed 29 December 2016).

70 Ibid.

71 Quoted in, "The Single Greatest Secret to Delivering a Perfect Presentation: Record Yourself Practicing." Online: https://www.panopto.com/blog/the-single-greatest-secret-to-delivering-a-perfect-presentation-record-yourself-practicing/ (accessed 29 December 2016).

72 John C. Maxwell, *Leadership Gold: Lessons from a Lifetime of Leading* (Nashville, TN: Thomas Nelson, 2008), 155.

73 Al Pittampalli, *Read This Before Our Next Meeting* (New York, NY: Portfolio, 2015), 27.

74 Patrick Lencioni, *The Advantage: Why Organizational Health Trumps Everything Else in Business* (San Francisco, CA: Jossey-Bass, 2012), 174.

75 Ibid., 175.

76 Lee Eclov, "Man Tries to Sue Himself," in *1001 Illustrations That Connect: Compelling Stories, Stats, and News Items for Preaching, Teaching, and Writing*, ed. Craig Brian Larson and Phyllis Ten Elshof (Grand Rapids, MI: Zondervan, 2008), 225.

77 Jim Collins, *How the Mighty Fall: And Why Some Companies Never Give In* (New York, NY: HarperCollins, 2011).

78 Fields, *Your First Two Years in Youth Ministry*, 45.

79 Amy Langfield, "Unused Vacation Days at 40-Year High." Online: http://www.cnbc.com/2014/10/23/unused-vacation-days-at-40-year-high.html (accessed 28 December 2016).

80 Ruth Haley Barton, *Strengthening the Soul of Your Leadership: Seeking God in the Crucible of Ministry* (Downers Grove, IL: InterVarsity Press, 2008), 62.

81 Frederick Buechner, *Listening to Your Life: Daily Meditations with Frederick Buechner* (New York, NY: HarperCollins, 1992), 186.

82 Os Guiness, *The Call: Finding and Fulfilling the Central Purpose of Your Life* (Nashville, TN: Thomas Nelson, 2003), 29.

83 Daily Mail UK, "One in 10 Families Never has an Evening Meal Together." Online: http://www.dailymail.co.uk/news/article-1323906/One-10-families-NEVER-evening-meal-together.html (accessed 1 January 2017).

84 Eugene Peterson, *Working the Angles: The Shape of Pastoral Integrity* (Grand Rapids, MI: Wm. B. Eerdmans, 1987), 73.

85 Walter Brueggemann, *Mandate to Difference: An Invitation to the Contemporary Church* (Louisville, KY: Westminster John Knox, 2007), 46.

86 Reggie Joiner, *A New Kind of Leader: What You Believe Can Open a Door for a Kid or Teenager's Future* (Atlanta, GA: Orange, 2016), 67.

87 Fields, *Your First Two Years in Youth Ministry*, 29.

88 Henry Cloud and John Townsend, *Boundaries: When to Say Yes, When to Say No to Take Control of Your Life* (Grand Rapids, MI: Zondervan, 1992), 33.

Made in the USA
San Bernardino, CA
28 August 2018